Praise for *Engage*

"*Finally*! A book that goes beyond the theology of community engagement to the concrete steps required to be in meaningful ministry with our congregation's neighbors. The strength of this book is its clear and easy-to-understand tools, which are practical and tested. Lay leaders and pastors will be encouraged by the accessibility of the many ways they can roll up their sleeves and begin (or deepen) the ministry they have always hoped for. Concrete examples of 'how to do it' are presented in every chapter. Based on years of field testing and the experiences of community advocates, these tools always yield good insights. Engaging with diverse communities has never been more challenging. But this book should encourage pastors and lay leaders that transforming community ministry is within their reach."

— Cynthia Woolever, coeditor, *The Parish Paper*

"As a high-school freshman far from home, Dana Horrell wanted to nourish his love of singing, an experience that reminded me of the ancient author of Psalm 137, living in exile in Babylon: 'How shall we sing the Lord's song in a foreign land?' The revolutionary answer to his question then was, 'Organize a synagogue!' In Dana's case the answer was, 'Join a church!' It was advice good for the centuries: 'make a congregation, and be sure it serves the needs of your new neighbors in this your new community.' In their welfare you will find your own.

Horrell has written a book full of practical suggestions not only for making a home in a new land but also for serving the needs of neighbors there. It is a book for mission-minded leaders of mission-dedicated congregations."

—Donald W. Shriver Jr., president emeritus,
Union Theological Seminary, New York City.

"*Engage!* is filled with practical tools that will help any congregation that is serious about getting more engaged with their community. Of particular note are the chapters that focus on helping church members get fully engaged in the process of developing and implementing new ministry—one of the more challenging aspects of the work."

—Joy Skjegstad, author, *7 Creative Models for Community Ministry* and *Starting a Nonprofit at Your Church*.

"In this era of tribalism and social fragmentation, practical theologian Dana Horrell speaks a wise pastoral word about the formative power of congregations to be the glue that binds together and strengthens their local community, giving folks a place to belong and flourish.

On every page of this book, Horrell draws on his deep familiarity with the field of congregational studies, providing church leaders with reliable information and actionable advice for cultivating 'faithful citizens' who live out their Christian discipleship on behalf of the common good. The tool kit Horrell hands us describes five practice clusters for community engagement: launching, building, mapping, supporting, and collaborating. These activities are artfully portrayed through short stories, modern parables that suggest ways we might adapt such practices for our own contexts.

—Don C. Richter, associate director, Louisville Institute

"Churches have lots of questions. One of them is: How do we engage people? This book reminds us of a better question. *Engage!* invites the church to ask how we engage ourselves in what God is doing in the lives of our neighbors. These practical steps can spin us around, and then there's no telling what wonders we will see and what adventures we will be invited to join."

—Mike Mather, pastor,
Broadway United Methodist Church

Engage!

Engage!

Tools for Ministry in the Community

Dana Horrell

Fortress Press
Minneapolis

ENGAGE!
Tools for Ministry in the Community

Cover design: Alisha Lofgren
Cover image: iStock / Rocks in a Circle by Silvrshootr

Print ISBN: 978-1-5064-5204-3
eBook ISBN: 978-1-5064-5205-0

The paper used in this publication meets the minimum requirements of American National Standard for Information Sciences — Permanence of Paper for Printed Library Materials, ANSI Z329.48-1984.

Manufactured in the U.S.A.

To Marti, ever faithful

Contents

Foreword

Over the years I have worked onsite as a ministry coach with around a thousand faith communities—churches of all sorts. Growing communities, aging communities, innovative communities, endangered communities, urban, rural, liberal, conservative, first-generation immigrant, and on and on. The common denominator across the board is that once the group agrees to a direction and to a plan, they easily get stuck at the most basic of exercises.

Getting stuck at the point of the basic "how to" is an equal-opportunity experience, especially with regard to community engagement and outreach. It occurs as often when half the team has a PhD as when half the team has a GED. Really smart folks get stuck. Every day. We are busy. Our knowledge and life wisdom are often specialized in work far beyond the task of developing new ministries and faith communities. We may look to the pastor for expertise, but friends, they don't teach much "how to" in seminary!

In the pages ahead, Dana Horrell provides us with an

immensely helpful resource, a handbook offering practical tips in the arena of "how to." He writes with a kindness toward the team member who missed the retreat, who wasn't present for the training, who didn't have time to "read the book," and who has limited experience in community outreach.

The chapters are short. The key concepts are chopped into bite-sized pieces. The material is simple but not simplistic. I would call it elegantly simple. He makes few assumptions. He helps us with the most basic concepts and practices in a way that is accessible to a wide audience. (Good preaching does this too, but I digress.)

You don't have to start at the beginning of the book. You can dive in at any point you have a question, and go from there. If you find a chapter that addresses a place where your team is stuck or needs help, three pages is short enough that you can just read it together in a team gathering, in minimal time, and then take action.

A few suggestions on how to use the book to your maximal benefit:

- If your church is cooking up a big, audacious idea or project that will require you to make a grant request of a denomination or foundation, consider doing a simple prototype of your big idea first—in part to test and refine it, and in part to build up your team's skill at executing community ministry initiatives. As you do your mini-project, your prototype, get a copy of *Engage!* for each person on your team. Such efforts will teach you volumes, so that when you write your grant application, you can demonstrate readiness to live into the vision that you are casting!

- If a particular chapter addresses a question where you are feeling stuck as a team, use that chapter as the primary agenda for your next team meeting, and you will experience the good fun of getting unstuck!
- As your ministry takes root and grows, you will need to develop leaders for the next generation of the ministry. (The lack of intentional leader development is the number one reason that ministries get stuck and fail to develop over time.) This book offers the kind of material that you will want to integrate into your ongoing leader-training process alongside the specific protocols and values that are particular to your church.
- Every desk or bookshelf needs a section reserved for the books we turn to often—Bibles, manuals, organizational rulebooks, and so forth. Put this book in that little collection. It will serve you best if you open it often. This is not a book with a few grand ideas that you digest once and then slip into your big collection of good books. You are going to need to find this one again and again.

The fact that you are even reading this page suggests that you are committed to taking ministry outside the church walls and into the community. I salute that! Best wishes and prayers to you and your team! Have fun. Let your neighbors teach you volumes and find ways to integrate them into the action. And soon you will be able to say, in the spirit of Luke 10, "The kingdom of God has come near!" Blessings on the adventures ahead!

Paul Nixon

Introduction

Millie, a member of the first church I served as pastor, had a droll sense of humor. "I used to play on a baseball team when I was younger," she told me once. "Oh?" I said. "What position did you play?" "Left out," she said. Millie's joke served as a commentary on the relationship between girls and institutional sports in her early years. In Millie's time, organized baseball offered a place of belonging for boys but left the other gender out. Little League baseball began permitting girls to play in 1974.

The case for community engagement begins here: it's not right to leave people out! Everyone needs a community, even though not everyone who lives in the neighborhood belongs to your church. No one should be left out or diminished through economic inequality, cultural marginalization, or other ways. Congregations can and must play a role in the survival of local communities. As Jesus commanded, "You shall love your neighbor as yourself" (Matt 22:39). This commandment applies to congregations as well as to individuals.

Starting high school in the early 1970s, I found myself thrust into a new faith community and wondering whether I belonged. As a freshman, I began attending St. John's United Methodist Church in Edwardsville, Illinois, a college town near St. Louis. We had just moved from Orlando, Florida, a thousand miles away, after my parents divorced and my mother decided it would be better for us to live closer to her parents. I wanted to sing, and the church had no youth choir, so I joined the adult choir. But did I belong?

Looking back years later, I realize that someone might have contested my place in the choir based on a definition of "adult." The day I arrived at choir, John Rider, my nearest neighbor in the bass section, welcomed me and showed me the ropes musically. Dr. Rider, a bearded, robust, gregarious man who served as professor and chair of the mass communications department at nearby Southern Illinois University, must have understood Jesus's commandment to love the neighbor as yourself. Or perhaps he sought to apply Jesus's teaching, "In everything do to others as you would have them do to you; for this is the law and the prophets" (Matt 7:12). Or perhaps he just wanted to share his love of music with someone much younger. Later, several choir members spoke glowingly to my mother, affirming that I belonged. Beyond singing, I became active in the youth group, served on committees, and took mission trips. I went from there to seek ordination in the United Methodist Church, and I kept singing.

We need strong communities where people belong, not just faith communities. We need strong local communities where we and our neighbors can flourish. When we engage our communities, we can strengthen them and improve the well-being of our neighbors. This engagement might include providing food, clothing, or cash; mentoring or starting a business incubator; removing tattoos from former gang members; throwing a party for public school teachers; community organizing or lobbying at the state capital; or any number of actions. Different denominations give it different names, including mission and outreach, home missions, social ministry, and justice ministry. Congregations can and must play a role. We need strong communities.

Though we need each other in order to flourish, American Christians often think otherwise. As Robert Bellah has observed, American individualism—that image of the lone individual seeking self-gratification—powerfully shapes how we experience ourselves.

> Individualism lies at the very core of American culture. . . . We believe in the dignity, indeed the sacredness, of the individual. Anything that would violate our right to think for ourselves, judge for ourselves, make our own decisions, live our lives as we see fit, is not only morally wrong, it is sacrilegious. Our highest and noblest aspirations, not only for ourselves, but for those we care about, for our society and the world, are closely linked to our individualism.[1]

Each of us wants to be a unique individual and to determine our own destiny. But here's a fact: we also need community

1. Robert Bellah et al., *Habits of the Heart* (Berkeley: University of California Press, 2008), 142.

in order to achieve personal fulfillment. It can be quite challenging to strike a balance between our individual needs and life in community. While our freedoms, rights, and liberties are indeed precious, we need to reexamine our individualism and see how faith and spirituality can be more deeply rooted in community. Bellah has pointed out the irony that American individualism, which keeps us separate, is at the same time a shared value that serves to hold American society together. Unfortunately, when individualism is overemphasized, it can lead to social isolation and economic inequality. Congregations offer a powerful counterbalance to such isolation.

Yet why not narrow our focus to building community within the congregation until we get it right? Why must we move outside the church walls to engage community? The answer lies in Jesus's commandment to love our neighbors as ourselves. When the Pharisees, the religious scholars of their day, challenged Jesus to establish his authenticity as a teacher of Mosaic law, he chose two commandments from the many hundreds of commandments listed in the Torah as centrally important. "He said to him, 'You shall love the Lord your God with all your heart, and with all your soul, and with all your mind.' This is the greatest and first commandment. And a second is like it: 'You shall love your neighbor as yourself.' On these two commandments hang all the law and the prophets" (Matt 22:37–40).

By linking the two commandments, Jesus claims that religious devotion is not enough. It must be accompanied by good works. By connecting the commandments to "the prophets," Jesus signals that love does not imply an emotional response so much as concern and action on behalf of neighbors near and far—and among friends as well as enemies. In other words, love for God requires concern and action for the common good. A true believer must also be a faithful citizen.[2] Likewise, the responsible congregation must seek the common good as well. Congregations, no matter where they are located, must try to reach outside their walls.

Recent data from the US Congregational Life Survey provides evidence of the church's failure to reach into neighborhoods. Cynthia Woolever, codirector of this survey, which reached nearly two thousand congregations nationwide, analyzed the extent to which congregations demographically match their surrounding communities. She concludes:

- Most congregations are less racially diverse than their surrounding neighborhoods.
- Only a few congregations (2 percent) are majority immigrant in a community with few immigrants.
- Young adults are vastly underrepresented in congregations compared with surrounding communities.
- They attract more worshippers aged forty-five to sixty-four years of age and a higher percentage of older worshippers than the surrounding community.

2. Nancy J. Duff, "The Second Great Commandment: Matthew 22:39–40," *Journal for Preachers*, Pentecost 2011, 18–23.

- They have more college-educated persons than the surrounding community.
- Of any demographic characteristic, the greatest mismatch was around the category of employment and unemployment. Fully 95 percent of congregations surveyed had more unemployed in the surrounding community than in church.[3]

Congregations can close this yawning gap by making an intentional effort to reach out and become better neighbors. There are so many possibilities. The National Congregations Study (NCS), a nationwide survey, provides data on congregation's activities, including engagement in the community. In order to grasp the full breadth of what American congregations do on this front, the researchers developed six broad categories of outreach.

1. Congregations can provide *social services* by participating in social-service programs, including community development and neighborhood projects. Congregations can offer programs providing food, housing, clothing, homelessness, or health care. They can invite representatives of social-service organizations as visiting speakers or hold a group meeting to organize or encourage people to do volunteer work.
2. Congregations can provide or support *education* for the community, and not just religious education. Some have

3. Cynthia Woolever and Deborah Bruce, *Places of Promise* (Louisville: Westminster John Knox, 2008), 63–64.

their own elementary school or high school, while others have given money to a college, university, or seminary or hosted a professor as visiting speaker. Some congregations hold small groups, educational programs, or mentoring programs whose purpose is education related.

3. Congregations can participate in dialogue or joint action in *religion* by holding a group or class to learn about another religion. Some congregations host clergy from another congregation as visiting speakers, or they participate in joint worship with another congregation from a religious tradition different from their own or with a racial or ethnic makeup different from their own.
4. Congregations can contribute to *culture* by hiring singers or other musicians to perform at a worship service, or by having visitors view the building's architecture or artwork. Some congregations organize a group or class to discuss a book other than the Bible. Others organize groups to attend a live musical or theatrical performance together, or they permit outside groups to use the building for rehearsals or performances of musical or theatrical works. Still other congregations invite groups to hold exhibits of paintings, photography, or sculpture in the building.
5. Congregations can decide as an institution to contribute to the *community*. This could be achieved by permitting outside groups to use or rent space in the building, or by holding a group or event to create and conduct an

assessment of community needs. Some congregations discuss vital community issues such as pollution or other environmental issues, or they discuss race relations in our society.

6. Though barred by law from supporting specific candidates and political parties, congregations can contribute to *politics* by holding a group meeting or event to discuss political issues. Likewise, they can organize or participate in efforts to lobby elected officials or take part in a demonstration or march about a public issue or policy. Congregations can also register people to vote, inform them at worship services about opportunities for political activity, or distribute voter guides. Some congregations get a political dialogue going by hosting an elected government official or someone running for office as a visiting speaker.[4]

Given the incredible variety of ways that congregations can engage the community—from providing social services to supporting education, to interfaith cooperation, to cultural contributions, to political action—it can be difficult to know how to proceed. Church leaders will need to think for themselves about what works best. That's where this book comes in.

This book offers a wide range of tools, which are methods or strategies for reaching out to the community, to help you

4. Mark Chaves, "Religious Variations in Public Presence: Evidence from the National Congregations Study," in *The Quiet Hand of God*, ed. Robert Wuthnow and John Evans (Berkeley: University of California Press, 2002), 108–28.

get started or to revitalize your work. Which resources you use will depend on what you hope to accomplish. That may be different depending on where you live and who your neighbors are.

Where do these tools come from? They derive from my work and the work of other consultants in churches large and small in the United States, and from a variety of church traditions, including mainline Protestant churches, the Roman Catholic Church, and the African American church. The tools also come from sociologists who have researched congregations that seek to engage their communities, which I did as part of a 2013 Pastoral Study Project funded by the Louisville Institute. The tools also come from six film shorts about church community engagement that I produced as part of a second Louisville Institute grant in 2015. These videos are accessible on my YouTube channel (search: Dana Horrell). Ideas for methods and strategies also come from my conversations with church leaders in my role as coeditor of *The Parish Paper*. They spoke with me about questions they faced or methods they used to solve problems.

The tools are grouped into five categories, which answer five basic questions church leaders might ask.

- How do we manage a community project, including how to get started? (*Administrative tools*)
- How do we think about our work before, during, and after our involvement? (*Reflective tools*)

- How can we get to know our community better? (*Mapping tools*)
- How can we build relationships, including with our own volunteers, through talk? (*Dialogue tools*)
- How can we expand our effectiveness through partnerships with others? (*Collaborative tools*)

Jesus's commandment "You shall love your neighbor as yourself" (Matt 22:39) sought to reduce the complexity of the Pharisaic interpretation of Torah law. To a great extent, he left it to his followers to determine what to do and how to do it. No matter what your community work, my hope is that these tools will help you. Nothing can be more frustrating than just starting a project and not knowing what to do next or reaching the awkward middle of your work and realizing you lack the knowledge or skill to accomplish what you set out to do. May these tools bring down the anxiety a notch or two and inspire you to keep going. May these tools strengthen your church's engagement, not only in the local neighborhood, but in the state, in the nation, and in the global community.

PART I

Administrative Tools

1

Determine the Problem to Be Solved

The world experiences its share of problems—hunger, joblessness, crime, environmental hazards—and you want to help. Yet be advised: it helps to get focused before jumping in with both feet. What problem needs to be solved? It makes sense to start locally in your community, the place where you live, work, or play. It also helps to be specific. Something needs to change! But wait. What should you do? Determining the problem to be solved becomes an essential first step.

It can be easy to get off track at the start of a project. Imagine Sophie, the new chair of First Church's mission and outreach committee, who wonders aloud what projects the group should tackle first. She decides to poll the other members for guidance. Andy, who loves gardening and has expertise at it, says, "Let's start a community garden!" Lucy, who has a talent for sewing, loves to shop secondhand, and has noticed new shops springing up around town, suggests starting a thrift shop. Someone else suggests raising money to give to local nonprofit agencies that benefit the poor and so forth. While none of these ideas are necessarily off track, the group has started at the wrong place. They should identify the problem at the outset instead of deciding what to do based on the resources on hand. First identify the problem to be solved. What in the community needs to change? Then ask, Are we the right people to do it? Do we have the resources?

Exclusive focus on resources can sidetrack a project, but so can focusing too heavily on people's immediate needs. While these needs certainly are important, other issues may be the cause of the real problems that need to be addressed! People may be hungry, yet the problem is not their hunger but something else, such as lack of jobs, transportation, or proper training. Along similar lines, try thinking in terms of "solving" rather than "helping," which is more appropriate to children. Sandra Swan, retired president of Episcopal Relief and Development, writes, "The helping that we decry is the helping that is an activity that masquerades as a solution to the problem. If we avoid using the term *help*, we will avoid falling into the trap of thinking that we have actually changed the system instead of merely smoothing over the symptom." This could be compared to a doctor treating the symptom without diagnosing the underlying cause.[1]

Staying focused on the problem can be challenging when so many demands clamor for attention. The Reverend Rod-

1. Sandra S. Swan, *The New Outreach* (New York: Church Publishing, 2011), 9.

ney Hunter, pastor of Wesley Memorial United Methodist Church in Richmond, Virginia, felt "constantly bombarded" by requests for emergency assistance and frustrated that providing cash assistance through the church's "mission fund" proved grossly inadequate. This small, predominantly African American church with 130 members sits squarely in the middle of a financially struggling neighborhood. "Our church is located in a community where there are many needs. We have three housing projects in our area. And, of course, with that, you have a lot of unemployment and low-wage earners. So, there are always needs. People always need utilities, rent, food, school clothing, and things of that nature."

Yet the emergency requests for aid masked a deeper problem: the ready availability of predatory loans. Due to lax state laws regulating the financial industry, storefront payday loan operations with names like Quick Cash and Cash Express had sprung up like mushrooms. Though promising relief from crushing debt, these loans were structured to trap unwary borrowers into paying annual interest rates as high as 300 or 400 percent. "Predatory lending is a problem," Hunter says, "because people go into it thinking it's not going to be difficult. It's usually a very small loan, but by the time you take out a two hundred–dollar loan and pay about a thousand dollars back, that's a problem."

The real problem was predatory loans, yet solving the problem required changing state laws, which would take too long and would not alleviate the immediate pain being created by massive debt. For this reason, Hunter, together with the Reverend Charles Swadley, approached the Virginia United Methodist Credit Union to develop the Jubilee Assistance Fund, which provides small-dollar loans (five hundred to a thousand dollars) at a reasonable and fair rate of interest to church members who are burdened by debt. The credit union provides the loan, while the church provides a small sum for collateral and promises to work with the church member, in one-on-one counseling, to develop a strategy to pay the loan back. "We still provide food or clothing when necessary. But we're concerned that it creates dependency. We want to help people help themselves."[2] By focusing on the problem to be solved, Hunter was able to get off the treadmill of activities related to providing cash assistance wherever it seemed necessary.

After determining the problem, capture it in a statement of purpose that encompasses the particulars of your situation. Some leaders come up with a mission statement for their team, but it can work for a program as well. The statement should say just enough without being overly comprehensive. A single-sentence statement may be too general to be useful. "Our mission is to educate the illiterate" may be accurate but too vague to be helpful. In crafting a statement, the goal you arrive at needs to relate to the local community, and it needs to be limited enough that you can accomplish it. St. Mary's Catholic Church in Alexandria, Virginia, wrote a mission statement that provides enough detail without being

2. Dana Horrell, "Compassionate Not Predatory," YouTube video, 7:26, May 10, 2017, https://tinyurl.com/ybmjhypc.

overly detailed: "The group probably most resistant to any social ministries is the group we want to target—parents with battered children. They have difficulty in parenting and lack identification of their needs. And they distrust help."[3] Developing a statement of purpose may seem like a waste of time, but it helps you avoid the dangers of "mission creep," an evocative term to describe how the objective of the project can become broadened and change in ways never anticipated.

The problem-solving approach to community engagement has its critics. For instance, an approach called asset-based community development prefers to start with the resources that a community needs rather than the problems that must be solved (see the "Develop Long-Term Partnerships" chapter). Both the needs-based and the problem-based approach have their merits. If you choose to begin with the problem, start by capturing it in a statement that encompasses the particulars of your situation. Be realistic about what you plan to do. These steps may keep your team on track early in the process. Otherwise, you may end up on a treadmill of activities without a clear goal.

3. Carl S. Dudley, *Community Ministry: New Challenges, Proven Steps to Faith-Based Initiatives* (Bethesda, MD: Alban Institute, 2002), 60.

For Reflection and Action

Here is a very simple three-step process to try:

1. Brainstorm issues and problems in your local community or neighborhood.
2. Determine which of the issues you wish to address.
3. Create a statement of purpose that defines the issue and what you hope to do about it.

2

Start a Project

It's time to start a project in the community. Where to start? Let's begin with a definition: a project is an activity that (1) has a specific objective, (2) has a start and end date, (3) may have funding limits, and (4) uses resources such as money, people, or equipment.[1] The important thing—and the definition makes this clear—is that projects are specific and limited. Being clear about what you want to accomplish (your specific objective), your time limit (your start and end date), and what sort of resources you will need (money, people, and equipment) can be make the task easier. Getting to your goal may be enormously complicated, but if it's a project, then by definition it will be time-limited. Whether it's a community garden, a food program, or arranging for children to visit their mothers in prison, it will start and end. It's important to keep that in mind at the outset.

1. R. E. Quinn, *Becoming a Master Manager* (Boston: Wiley & Sons, 2003), 139.

How do you get started? The following seven steps may clear away enough of the confusion to get you into the action. Following the exact order of steps may be less important than getting a sense of the basic pieces. When in doubt, start somewhere, and then do something after that.[2]

Step 1: Have a Clear Goal

It helps to start this community project with a clear goal or statement of purpose (see the previous chapter). What do you want to accomplish? What results do you want? What in the community needs to change? Many people will engage in a series of activities with no clear sense of what results they want. Whenever possible, identify the root causes of the problem. Hunger persists in your neighborhood despite the fact that most families are working. Why? What is the underlying problem? This could be compared to a doctor diagnosing the underlying cause instead of simply treating the symptom.[3]

Step 2: Do Research

For some people, the word *research* brings to mind a lonely, isolated process of bringing together dry facts about the situation. Yet the most effective research is relational. You can do research by meeting one to one with community leaders and building deeper relationships with a few of them by meeting

2. Adapted from Benjamin Shepard, *Community Projects as Social Activism* (Thousand Oaks, CA: Sage, 2015), 3.
3. Sandra S. Swan, *The New Outreach* (New York: Church Publishing, 2010), 2–14.

on a regular basis, such as monthly or quarterly. You can do research by attending community events or participating in community groups that convene regularly, volunteering in the community, taking a walk around the neighborhood, or going door to door in the community, assuming this is safe and that people would respond well to this approach.[4]

Step 3: Communicate

Now it is time to make a case for the project and recruit volunteers to help you with it. Best practices include developing a purpose statement for the project, creating a recognizable logo to remind people of your project, and coming up with "sound bite" to sum up the spirit of what you're doing.

Step 4: Put Together a Team

In one way of looking at it, effective projects always start in the mind of an individual. A thought, a dream, or a snatch of conversation might be just the spark that gets the fire going. Yet even when it starts with a person, the fire rarely burns long or well enough without the help of others. Normally, it takes a team to provide the structure and to fuel that initial spark. A team has been defined as "a small group of people with complementary skills who are committed to a common purpose, performance goals and approach for which they are mutually accountable."[5] As the definition suggests,

4. Joy F. Skjegstad, 7 *Models for Community Ministry* (Valley Forge, PA: Judson, 2013), 17–26.
5. Jon R. Katzenbach, *The Wisdom of Teams* (San Francisco: HarperBusiness, 1994), 12.

the group needs to be small enough to make effective decisions together, yet diverse enough, based on "complementary skills," so that the group's strengths can build on one another. Members must also work together with a "common purpose" and be "mutually accountable" for what they do. Regarding diversity, try searching for these four types: (1) an *investor* who provides resources such as time, talent, or money to the project; (2) an *intermediary* who "acts as a bridge between an investor and the program implementers"; (3) an *implementer* who does the hands-on work; and (4) an *innovator* who "dream[s] up new ways to solve problems."[6]

Of course, you may already serve on a standing committee or team. Even so, consider expanding the group by inviting newer members of the congregation or those not yet actively involved. Reach out also to your circle of friends outside the church. In my consulting, I am struck at how many times volunteers feel called first and foremost to outreach, even before participating in worship, though sometimes this may change over time. It helps to keep an open mind about who will serve on your team. Email or social media can be used to get the word out, though for some people, word of mouth still works best.

Step 5: Take Action

At some point, you need to make the leap. For some reason, this can be more difficult for groups than individuals. Con-

6. Swan, *New Outreach*, 61–63.

gregations can find it difficult to be bold. In a book providing examples of bold ministries, Linda Marie Delloff observes that the most successful ones are able to "recognize, then overcome their fears, or at least they are willing to take risks despite their fears." Fears include failure, rejection by the targeted public, physical or emotional discomfort, or even physical danger. It can also include fear of "the other," that is, people who are different than oneself. She writes, "Such congregations are willing, even eager, to accept these risks because they know that by always being 'safe' they will never change anything."[7]

Step 6: Find Ways to Expand on Your Action

A project usually starts with a single action, such as collecting food for the hungry, but over time you may want to expand on it by finding additional ways to achieve the same end. Have you thought of adding fresh food by asking donations from local gardens? Have you thought of teaching nutrition or cooking? Have you thought of asking food recipients to volunteer for you? Have you thought of holding a community discussion on what causes hunger and how to change policy? These ideas serve as variations on the theme of hunger, and new actions may help the project expand.

7. Linda-Marie Delloff, *Public Offerings: Stories from the Front Lines of Community Ministry* (Bethesda, MD: Alban Institute, 2002), 14.

Step 7: Use Sustainability Strategies to Keep It Going

Often people burn out because they have not thought about sustainability strategies. This may include sharing a special meal together to celebrate accomplishments and people, using small-group Bible study as a place to reflect on your action, inviting the people you serve to pray with you, or developing a Sunday worship service centered on a social issue. Sustainability can be as much about mental and spiritual capacity as about finances or volunteer hours. Studying, sharing meals, celebrating—these are sustainability strategies. Do them, or something like them, and you will never burn out.

Framing your community project as a series of steps can sharpen focus. When done effectively, such projects can make a big difference by addressing directly the problems you and your neighbors face every day.

3

Recruit Volunteers

Working with others can be stressful and complicated, so it may be tempting to go it alone. Yet is self-reliance any better? Recruiting and equipping others to work with you builds relationships with others in our midst. If the goal of our work is to strengthen community, solo performance would not seem the best choice to achieve that end. It makes more sense to use a team.

Of course, some churches rely on solo actors to do their community engagement. Rich Fowler, social action director of the Archdiocese of Washington of the Roman Catholic Church, describes a tour he made of parishes in the archdiocese. He asked the pastor of a medium-sized parish, "Do you have a social concerns committee here?" The priest responded, "Oh, you mean Bertha! Bertha's great! She would be a big help to you! I don't know what I'd do without Bertha!"[1] Unfortunately, the solo actor may rob others of the opportunity to get involved. How can we learn unless we take part?

Instead of getting "Bertha" to do all the work, McEachern Memorial United Methodist Church in Powder Springs, Georgia, developed teams. The church developed its Car Care Ministry to address the problem of low-income and elderly people unable to maintain their cars. The ministry centers around its volunteers. One Thursday evening and one Saturday morning each month, volunteer mechanics bring cars into an old barn out in the country. The team does routine maintenance work for elderly and lower-income car owners, such as replacing oil, filters, belts, and bulbs, and they also donate vehicles to repair and give to people in need. While patrons are asked to pay the cost of parts if they are able, labor is provided free of charge. The Car Care Ministry could not function without its teams, and church leaders offer multiple places where people can get involved: donating a vehicle or basic supplies, working as a mechanic or parts runner who goes out to shop for supplies, or serving as a "lounge angel" who chats with patrons waiting for repairs or brings breakfast for workers and patrons.[2] By multiplying the number of entry points for volunteers, the church builds community as it repairs cars.

How do you set up a system for recruiting volunteers? Start by considering the journey a new member makes from sit-

1. Jeffry Odell Korgen, *My Lord and My God: Engaging Catholics in Social Ministry* (New York: Paulist Press, 2007), 17.
2. McEachern Memorial United Methodist Church, "Local Outreach," https://tinyurl.com/y848atfy.

ting in the pews on Sunday morning to getting involved in the congregation's ministries. The process ideally would involve six steps: (1) being assimilated into membership through a new member process; (2) learning about the biblical basis for service through preaching and teaching; (3) exploring one's personal passions and gifts through a "discovery" interview; (4) being asked to serve in a volunteer position; (5) getting equipped to serve through training, feedback, and evaluation; and (6) being replenished and sustained in this ministry through public recognition and private reflection.[3]

The third step, discovery of a person's passions and gifts, is at the heart of an effective volunteer system. Arrange a one-on-one interview, ask open-ended questions, and practice reflective listening in order to discover the abilities, interests, gifts, motivations, temperament, skills, and life experiences of potential volunteers. Sample questions might include:

- I would be interested in learning about your family. Tell me about . . .
- What do you do (or have you done) to earn your livelihood?
- What do you love doing?
- What do you dislike doing and hope never to have to do again?

3. Sue Mallory and Brad Smith, *The Equipping Church Handbook* (Grand Rapids: Zondervan, 2001), 244–346.

- We seldom have the opportunity to share with others those things that we most enjoyed and felt we did well. What things have you accomplished that you are really proud of?[4]

Take prolific notes or use a prefabricated form to capture information. Some congregations use volunteer database software for its members, which is fine as long as confidentiality is respected regarding personal issues that might arise in the interview. Listen not only for positive factors but also for reasons why this might not be the best time for the person to volunteer due to burnout from previous service, personal crisis, or major life transition.

To be most effective and caring, the discovery step must come first, prior to matching someone with a volunteer position. To understand this principle, think what is required for a successful volunteer placement: a good fit between the person's gifts and the job to be done. Asking someone to serve in a specific role before knowing their gifts risks a situation in which the volunteer discovers, to their dismay, that they cannot perform the job adequately or do not feel motivated to do it. By starting with an open-ended discovery interview not tied to any matching possibilities, church leaders demonstrate a concern with helping others flourish, not simply getting jobs done. Such a focus shows appreciation and caring. In the worst case, the interviewer has asked a fellow church member to talk about their gifts and passions and later discovers no immediate matches with a relevant volunteer position.

4. Mallory and Smith, *Equipping Church*, 287–88.

Nevertheless, the interview subject has been asked to tell their story in the presence of someone who listens and cares. It is truly a win-win situation.

Community projects are best undertaken together. That is not to rule out serving the community by volunteering individually for a program sponsored by a local agency outside the church. In this case, it pays to keep track of those who volunteer, share the news of their work with others in the congregation, and count the solo volunteer's service when measuring the church's ministry. By doing so, congregations affirm that those who volunteer on their own outside the walls of the church are still doing the church's work. For those who choose to volunteer as part of the congregation's outreach programs, an effective recruiting system brings these persons on board so they can experience the benefits of working in community.

4

Equip Volunteers

At its most basic level, equipping volunteers means supporting their work in order to sustain their activity over time. The apostle Paul calls on leaders "to equip the saints for the work of ministry, for the building up of the body of Christ" (Eph 4:12), which indicates that as we prepare others (equipping), we make them and other believers (the body of Christ) stronger and stronger (building up). The metaphor is both positive and growth oriented. The process of equipping has multiple aspects.

Orientation

The volunteer should be provided with a job description laying out what they will be doing.[1] An orientation program goes beyond the job description by offering an introduction

1. See Marlene Wilson, *Volunteer Job Descriptions and Action Plans*, vol. 3, *Group's Volunteer Leadership Series* (Loveland, CO: Group, 2004) for detailed instruction on how to design job descriptions.

to what it will be like for the volunteer once the work begins. An effective orientation can reinforce the volunteer's initial decision to get involved, provide a connection with the wider purpose of the program, and reduce volunteer turnover. Of course, the orientation also should provide information a new volunteer will need. If you are unclear what to include, ask several of the more experienced volunteers for their opinion.[2]

Volunteer Handbook

At the orientation, plan to distribute a volunteer handbook. This book provides information about procedures and policies that may have been reviewed verbally in the orientation but may not be readily remembered due to information overload. Policies provide general guidance for what is expected of the volunteer on the job. For example, youth mission volunteers need to agree to a policy of never having an adult with a minor in a car alone. Procedures, by contrast, have to do with practical guidance on how to get the job done. For example, volunteers may need to be told the best procedure for lining up a substitute volunteer in case of sickness. In addition to policies and procedures, the handbook can include areas such as the ministry's purpose and values, organizational structure, and dress codes; safety and security information; and how the work will be evaluated.

2. Marlene Wilson, *Volunteer Orientation and Training*, vol. 5, *Group's Volunteer Leadership Series* (Loveland, CO: Group, 2004), 9–19.

Training Session

Nearly all volunteer positions require some sort of training, which might be anything from an informal conversation about how to operate that outdated office copy machine to a detailed set of instructions for volunteers canvassing the neighborhood door to door. If you plan to hold a training session, first determine the need. Some experts refer to this practice as "gap analysis" because it involves identifying the space between what people know and what they need to know. As any classroom teacher would do, write a few learning objectives for your students. What can you realistically accomplish by the end of the session? Next try writing a class outline. Some trainers might regard an outline as a creativity killer, but it need not be so. Having a sequence of steps prepared ahead of time can lend confidence and cure unexpected jitters that may arise once the training session begins. Spontaneity can still occur within structure. Be sure to practice ahead of time by walking through the session, paying attention to the timing of the activities and thinking about how you will set up the location where the training will take place. Finally, ask for feedback from students through a simple evaluation near the end of the session.[3]

3. Wilson, *Volunteer Orientation and Training*, 55–69. For a sample evaluation form, see p. 101.

Setting Expectations

Expectations, defined as "our assumptions about the future—how we anticipate things will go," can often determine whether the volunteer has a worthwhile experience.[4] Be clear with your volunteers about your expectations. Assume volunteers want to do their best and that it may be your own failure to communicate that is at fault whenever expectations are not met. Tell the volunteer not just what is to be done but how it is to be done. Every three to six months, ask, "What do you need from me that you're not getting?" and also "What do you wish to know about your volunteer job that you don't know?"[5]

Evaluation

There are two types of evaluation that must be done: evaluating the ministry itself and evaluating the volunteers as individuals. Evaluation and planning are closely connected. You must develop a mission statement and strategic plan in order to evaluate it later. Did you accomplish what you set out to do within the timeline you set out and within budget?[6]

Evaluating your volunteers as individuals constitutes the second task, one that allows them to find out how they are doing. This does not have to be a challenging time,

4. Marlene Wilson, *Volunteer Encouragement, Evaluation, and Accountability,* vol. 6, *Group's Volunteer Leadership Series* (Loveland, CO: Group, 2004), 9.
5. Wilson, *Volunteer Encouragement,*17.
6. For more detail on planning and evaluating programs, see Kathleen A. Cahalan, *Projects That Matter: Successful Planning and Evaluation for Religious Organizations* (Lanham, MD: Rowman & Littlefield, 2014).

but rather it can be affirming and celebratory. Performance reviews offer an opportunity for the leader who assigned the job and the volunteer who performs it to talk about how things are going. It is important to schedule such meetings on a regular basis. Marlene Wilson sums up the attitude that leaders should take toward evaluation: “Performance reviews should be nonthreatening, constructive, supportive, flexible, and empowering. The aim: to encourage volunteers to stretch for high standards and determine how the church can help the volunteer achieve his or her goals.”[7]

Recognition

Leaders provide encouragement when they recruit volunteers well, place them carefully, and evaluate their performance in a healthy way. In addition to this, leaders can and should formally recognize the volunteer’s contribution. It’s not possible to offer too much appreciation! While we tend to think of recognition as occurring at the end of a project, recognition should take place throughout the volunteer experience. Betty Stallings, a recognition expert, describes the “Four Ps” of recognition: make it *personal*, *plentiful*, *powerful*, and *practical*.

Making it personal means crafting a thank you that validates the person in a way unique to them. For instance, one organization sent its staff members a card of recognition on the anniversary of the date they started working there.

7. Wilson, *Volunteer Encouragement,* 67.

Making it plentiful means, like the old joke about voting in Chicago, doing it early and often. Doing so can help spread the attitude of recognition throughout your work team. Making it powerful means recognizing the importance of small symbolic acts, such as the conference organizer who drew out of her pocket a partial roll of Lifesavers at the end of the meeting, handed one to her most trusted assistant, and said, "You've been a real Lifesaver today!"[8] Making it practical means addressing the excuses people make for not providing recognition, most of them centered on its alleged impracticality. For instance, some will protest about the lack of money in the budget or observe that volunteers say they do not need recognition. To counter these objections, point out the ways in which recognition sustains the work by encouraging everyone involved.[9]

Equipping volunteers is a process, not a program. This tool is too complex to be encapsulated neatly in a short space.[10] As the apostle Paul's metaphor implies, maintaining a healthy body of volunteers requires an ongoing effort of nourishment and support. The more continual the encouragement and support, the stronger the body grows in its ministry to the community.

8. Wilson, *Volunteer Encouragement,* 91.
9. Wilson, *Volunteer Encouragement*, 83–92.
10. To go deeper into this subject, see Wilson, *Group's Volunteer Leadership Series*, or Sue Mallory and Brad Smith, *The Equipping Church Handbook* (Grand Rapids: Zondervan, 2001). For general resources on working with volunteers, see the website of Energize, Inc., a training, consulting, and publishing firm specializing in volunteerism, at www.energizeinc.com.

5

Fund Your Work

A community project consists of someone's idea or dream, a plan designed by a core team, and a group of volunteers willing to roll up their sleeves and get to work. Yet how can this worthy work be sustained over time? Whether the project involves food, clothing, housing assistance, counseling and job training, or organizing residents around an issue of local importance such as the need for a community garden or more stop signs, at some point the program might require funding in order to continue.

In order to raise money effectively, leaders must develop a plan for future spending, that is, a budget. Some leaders prefer to build long-range planning into their thinking at the outset. The Reverend Constance Delzell, rector of St. Andrew's Episcopal Church in Denver, decided to factor the necessity for funding into her dream of a children's ministry for the community. She describes waking from a dream, which she believes was divinely inspired, telling her that now was the time to take action on her wish to start an arts ministry. Based on this vision, she founded the Children's Center for Arts and Learning, a neighborhood ministry serving a low-income community in the city of Denver. From the beginning, she began developing a plan for sustainability. She thinks that many congregations often make a mistake by failing to plan for their project's financial future. Because St. Andrew's was small with few resources, she approached members of previous churches she had served who she thought might be interested and have financial means. Then a personal friend provided ten thousand dollars in seed money over three years. At this point, she took some of the total received to hire a secretary and part-time grant writer. Thinking strategically helped the program move from vision to funding.[1]

As this example illustrates, individual giving can play an important role in fundraising efforts. In fact, a vast majority of funding for nonprofits originates from individuals, not foundations. In 2017, foundations provided only about 15 percent of all donations to US nonprofits, while 72 percent originated with individuals.[2] With this in mind, keep your eyes on the prize by reaching out to both close ties and community members, letting foundations take a secondary role. Basing a budget strategy on individual gifts can provide more stability than funding from foundations, whose priorities tend to change every few years.

1. Linda-Marie Delloff, *Public Offerings: Stories from the Front Lines of Community Ministry* (Bethesda, MD: Alban Institute, 32–33.
2. "Giving USA 2017: Total Charitable Donations Rise to New High of 0.05 Billion," Giving USA, June 12, 2017, https://tinyurl.com/yaz298xg.

Joy Skjegstad, who advises churches on their community ministry programs, suggests starting with church members who already have the strongest connection with the project, including volunteers currently working in the program or previous volunteers. Meet with potential donors face to face and ask for a specific amount, following up with written materials (no more than one or two pages long) that describe the project's mission and activities and various amounts that could be given. Make sure to follow up, which could be as simple as sending a brochure or program budget.

Asking church members may be complicated by the fact that other appeals are being made at the same time of the year for some other worthy cause. For this reason, try to schedule funding appeals with the church funding schedule in mind. Check with the pastor or staff to avoid inadvertently blind-siding other ministries. When possible, coordinate with others. Skjegstad tells of one scheduling conflict that required just such coordination. While working on the church staff, she sought to make a funding appeal for the nonprofit she directed, which had close ties to the church. Her group's appeal sought funding for a health clinic and a tutoring and computer-training center. Yet at the same time, the church's food pantry was making a funding appeal for Christmas food baskets, and the trustees had launched a drive to fund special "fix-it" projects. All three appeals happened at that prime time in the church's life: the end of the year. After some discussion, the three groups decided to coordinate their appeals, making joint announcements from the pulpit three weeks in a row and providing bulletin inserts with all three appeals listed together.[3]

Church leaders can take the idea of joint fundraising to a new level through planning a "Miracle Sunday" offering. The Miracle Sunday approach utilizes a strategy found in a variety of annual stewardship campaigns: an extensively planned campaign culminating in a single, celebratory event in which church members make their offerings at the Sunday worship service and tabulate the results that same day. As with other stewardship campaigns, Miracle Sunday relies on a team of people with strong financial giving records, a promotional campaign built up over a period of weeks (twelve weeks is recommended), and an explicitly stated and ambitious financial goal. However, unlike most stewardship campaigns, Miracle Sunday focuses not on the overall budget but on one to three worthy causes, such as community projects, building improvement, or music or education that benefit church members. Another difference between Miracle Sunday and traditional stewardship campaigns is that donors are asked to give not from current income but from their accumulated resources, such as savings, stocks, or the sale of other valuable items such as cars, boats, or real estate.

A Miracle Sunday campaign typically lasts about twelve weeks and takes place in the spring so as not to interfere with the fall stewardship campaign. The planning team sends four mailings spread over several weeks, holds two informational

3. Joy F. Skjegstad, 7 *Models for Community Ministry* (Valley Forge, PA: Judson, 2013), 177–81.

meetings, and makes a series of worship service announcements. No home visits are required. The goal for the Miracle Sunday is a single offering that exceeds anything the church has given before (hence the name, "Miracle Sunday").

To make it most effective, set an ambitious goal, usually at least one third of the church's annual budget. Herb Miller states, "Miracle Sunday has raised an amount equal to between one-third and three times the size of the church's annual operating budget in countless congregations across the United States." He observes that congregations that experienced a budget shortfall in the previous year are surprised at the success of their Miracle Sunday campaign the following year, which may be due to the fact that contributions come from accumulated resources and may even represent a once-in-a-lifetime gift. For that reason, Miracle Sunday should not be relied on as a yearly event but used sparingly.[4]

Providing funds can help community-engagement work grow and thrive. When projects reach a certain size, fundraising may provide an answer to previously insurmountable challenges, such as maintaining volunteer involvement, acquiring needed equipment, or ensuring enough space to make it all work. While funding should never be considered an end in it itself, it helps keep the lights on, pays the bills, and keeps the program thriving. Funding often is key to future sustainable success.

4. Herb Miller, "Planning and Leading a Miracle Sunday Campaign," *The Parish Paper*, https://tinyurl.com/y6v98arg.

6

Build Capacity

Capacity has to do with the amount of resources in hand. For churches, capacity could be reflected in the number of members, size of the budget, number of buildings, amount of land, funding, number of volunteers, or equipment supporting its programs. Organizational theorists describe organizations or programs with a relatively high degree of "slack" as robust. Imagine a large, well-stocked supermarket on the eve of a hurricane whose stock gets utilized as the crowds converge on the store to fill their pantries. Normally a convenience store would do just as well, but with the storm coming in, the supermarket seems more likely to have everything buyers need.

Failure to pay attention to capacity can have disastrous consequences. In a workshop we taught together on equipping churches for outreach, the Reverend Roderic Frohman, a Presbyterian Church (USA) pastor in Rochester, New York, described a worst-case scenario:

> A couple of years ago at Third Presbyterian Church, our Saturday noon lunch program had a glut of unexpected visitors, probably double the eighty people we usually feed every Saturday noon. We later learned that a neighboring social service agency, which held a Saturday lunch at exactly the same time, had shut down for a month in order to repair their facilities. The ten volunteers who served the lunch that Saturday were completely overwhelmed. Worried about not getting enough food, two guests began to fight, duking it out on a table, which fell on an elderly lady, breaking her hip. Pandemonium reigned, the police and an ambulance were called, order was restored, but our volunteers were significantly rattled.[1]

The breakdown is simple to explain: a sudden surge in demand had overwhelmed capacity. A lunch program equipped to serve eighty persons experienced an influx of 160. The result was a food fight.

In the case of Third Presbyterian's lunch program, robustness might have to do with any number of factors in addition to a hearty soup, such as (1) having more than enough volunteers (2) with ample training (3) serving an abundance of food (4) according to guidelines, which are published in a clear, easy-to-read handbook (5) with an appendix telling you what to do when emergencies happen.

What about individuals? Here capacity has to do with the amount of time, energy, or ability to get the job done. We know why volunteers burn out. Running a program that offers food or clothing assistance can feel so unrelenting. How can program leaders build capacity when the needs are so overwhelming? Remember the adage: take time to sharpen

1. Roderic P. Frohman, presentation for "Equipping the Congregation for Outreach and Mission," Trinity Episcopal Church, Seattle, Washington, October 26, 2013.

the saw. As the saw becomes dull, the woodcutter or home builder may find the project imperceptibly slowing down. When this dulling happens to individuals, we call it burnout. What is burnout? It seems to have been coined by Graham Greene's *A Burnt-Out Case*. In this novel, the main character writes in his journal: "I haven't enough feeling left for human beings to do anything for them out of pity." Jennifer Senior, in an article for *New York Magazine*, observes, "People who are suffering from burnout often describe it in terms of emptiness—they're a dry teapot over a high flame, a drained battery that can no longer hold its charge."[2] It can happen to volunteers.

Greenpoint Reformed Church in Brooklyn answered a crisis of morale among its volunteers by shutting its lunch program down temporarily. Serving a predominantly poor neighborhood with a poverty rate of 36 percent, the church found its food pantry and lunch program overwhelmed by a rising tide of clients. Worried about running out of food and funding and saddened by the death of the chef and the departure of a college-student intern, the pastor made a drastic decision: the program would temporarily shut down. For two months during the summer, the program closed its doors. Suddenly there was time to build capacity! Volunteers cleaned out the kitchen and brought it up to code, visited other food pantries to learn best practices, and drafted a set of volunteer guidelines. The result? Some volunteers got angry

2. Jennifer Senior, "Can't Get No Satisfaction," *New York Magazine,* October 24, 2007, https://tinyurl.com/yc5q8fbu.

and quit. Clients were forced to go elsewhere, and when it reopened, they did not immediately come back. Yet happily, volunteers and staff discovered a newfound sense of joy in their work. The Reverend Ann Kansfield remarked, "I love being around on Wednesdays and Thursdays now. I never would have thought that managing a soup kitchen requires every last ounce of skill and brains that I have. It is the hardest thing I've ever done."[3] It took courage to shut down operations temporarily, but it rejuvenated the program.

What if you lack sufficient capacity to organize a project of your own and do not expect to get it anytime in the near future? In this case, try collaborating with a social service agency by providing them with volunteers from your church. You can still count this as your ministry when you report on your activities. Collaborating allows you to broaden the impact of your work without squeezing resources. Doing so makes it possible for congregations to have a larger impact than they otherwise would have besides practicing more efficient pooling of resources. Social-service agencies provide a certain level of professionalism unavailable to volunteer groups working on their own.

Building capacity not only increases church leaders' ability to respond to crisis, but it can create a higher sense of morale as volunteers feel more effective and better able to accomplish what they set out to do. Having ample capacity increases the likelihood of an enduring ministry. For example, con-

3. Genine Babikian, "A Brooklyn Church Temporarily Shuts Down Its Hunger Ministry in Order to Sustain It," Faith and Leadership, https://tinyurl.com/yd43soob.

gregations that regularly integrate social concerns into prayer and worship and regularly take the time to affirm the service of members are less likely to experience a dramatic ebb and flow of community-engagement activities. They take time to sharpen the saw.

PART II

Reflective Tools

7

Prepare through Study

Standing on the verge of action, why take the time to study? Why not just roll up your sleeves and get to work? The immediate problem with this scenario can be unexpected misfires—outcomes we had hoped to avoid and frustrations we would rather not deal with. We might have saved time in the long run by taking time at the outset to study.

In some cases, study may serve to overcome a congregation's passivity about social action based on a misreading of the church's role in society. Sociologist Robert Bellah notes an American tendency to privatize religion based on a misunderstanding of the separation of church and state. Many people misread the First Amendment's disestablishment clause, thinking it forbids religious involvement in political life, when its true goal is to protect religion from government interference. The idea of separating religion from public life gained such ground over time that by the early nineteenth century, "privatization placed religion, together with the family, in a compartmentalized sphere that provided loving support but could no longer challenge the dominance of utilitarian values in the society at large."[1] Church leaders can counter this tendency by studying the Bible's social ethics. Study can provide a corrective to misunderstanding.

For instance, both Bruce Birch and Richard Bauckham treat the Bible's ethical significance for personal and public life while Norman Wirzba argues for the ethical relevance of the doctrine of creation for responding to the ecological crisis.[2]

Unfortunately, many mainline Protestant churches do not expend much energy on the study of their faith traditions. Sociologist Nancy Ammerman has found the mainline Protestant church weak in the area of adult faith formation. Most congregations, mainline or not, have at least one study or prayer group, yet less than half (40 percent) of them hold any classes during "prime time" on Sunday morning before or after worship. Overall, mainline churches set a low bar of expectation for adult education compared to conservative Protestant and African American churches. In addition, only 14 percent of mainline churches offer regular classes for new members, even though half of their members grew up in other denominations.

1. Robert Bellah et al., *Habits of the Heart: Individualism and Commitment in American Life* (Berkeley: University of California Press, 2008), 224.
2. Bruce C. Birch, *Let Justice Roll Down: The Old Testament, Ethics, and the Christian Life* (Louisville: Westminster John Knox, 1991); Richard Bauckham, *The Bible in Politics: How to Read the Bible Politically* (Louisville: Westminster John Knox, 2011); Norman Wirzba, *The Paradise of God: Renewing Religion in an Ecological Age* (New York: Oxford University Press, 2003).

By paying so little attention to adult education, less than any other American faith group, "white Mainline Protestants seem to be putting all their eggs in the basket of morning worship and children's Sunday school." Why? Unlike other groups such as Catholics or Jews, mainline Protestants do not see themselves as outsiders to American culture. For much of American history, they were the leaders in education, government, and business, so they have felt less need to reinforce the basics of the faith.[3]

To make adult education and Bible study more central to church life, try offering a variety of classes on the Bible throughout the year, not just during Lent and Advent, and scheduling more classes mid-week in order to allow more time for in-depth study. Class leaders wanting to link Bible study to community engagement can use downloadable resources offered through Faithlink, a United Methodist Church curriculum, The Thoughtful Christian, a similar curriculum of the Presbyterian Church (USA), or Dialogues On . . . (Sparkhouse). The downloads typically cover a single topic per session. Topics in these resources include migration, migrant children, the workplace, nuclear waste, homelessness, gun control, food production and consumption, recycling, and civility. Fortress Press has published a helpful little book titled *Faith in Action: A Handbook for Activists, Advocates, and Allies.* A six-session Lenten curriculum by The Thoughtful Christian on faith and community engagement, *Faithful*

3. Nancy Ammerman, *Pillars of Faith: American Congregations and Their Partners* (Berkeley: University of California Press, 2005), 272–73.

Citizen: Living Responsibly in a Global Society, is scheduled to be available in 2019.[4] From time to time, the preacher could supplement the sermon by assigning a Bible passage for the whole congregation to study in the coming week.[5]

In addition to Bible study, consider studying the congregation's particular history. Ask how the community project you are about to start aligns with the congregation's unique identity. Carl Dudley notes the impatience of some mission and outreach teams. "Some committees never listen, but always talk, trying to persuade the congregation with a sales pitch for their idea."[6] Slow the process down by exploring congregational identity first. How does your church use the Bible in worship music, spoken prayers, or sermons, or when critical decisions must be made? What creeds, doctrines, and denominational policy statements does the church treasure? What heroes and heroines are celebrated from your past? What church stories are told repeatedly about the church's ethnic-cultural journey, its location, or its service to or insulation from the world?[7]

Church leaders can integrate a time for study with an "immersion experience" to learn more about a particular community. Journey to Justice, a weekend retreat designed for Roman Catholic parishes, combines study of the Bible and Catholic social teaching with a community tour guided by

4. To see these resources, go to www.cokesbury.com/faithlink; www.thethoughtfulchristian.com; www.wearesparkhouse.org; and www.fortresspress.com.
5. Dick Murray, *Teaching the Bible to Adults and Youth* (Nashville: Abingdon, 1993), 21–22.
6. Carl S. Dudley, *Community Ministry* (Hernden, VA: Alban, 2002), 66.
7. Dudley, *Community Ministry*, 63–104.

local leaders. On Friday evening participants learn about "the preferential option for the poor" and the concept of social sin (unjust systems that oppress the poor). On Saturday morning the group studies the parable of the good Samaritan, with its focus on serving neighbors who are radically different from us. In the afternoon the group visits a social agency, hearing from one of "the empowered poor" in the community, who serves as their guide. In debriefing that evening, participants share what they experienced and felt during the visit, revisit church teachings, and examine the root causes of poverty. The retreat ends on Sunday morning with a guided imagery exercise and later with a Mass in which participants are invited to commit to follow-up action. In this example, study of the Bible and social teachings provides a theological context for the immersion experience.[8]

Study can serve as a catalyst for action. The town of Comanche, Oklahoma, experienced economic hardship after the closing of two factories. In a school system serving five towns and one thousand students, a majority of children were eligible for a federal free-meal program twice per day. First Church, a small church with only fifty members, began studying Matthew 25:31–46, the Great Judgment in which Christ's followers are separated into sheep and goats based on how they treat others. Church leaders asked, "How can a church find Christ in a town that has lost hope?" They also read the Great Commission in Matthew 28:16–20, with

8. Jeffry Odell Korgen, *My Lord and My God: Engaging Catholics in Social Ministry* (New York: Paulist, 2007), 55–71; *Journey to Justice Guidebook* (Washington, DC: US Conference of Catholic Bishops, 2014), https://tinyurl.com/y9wnbjgt.

its commandment to make disciples, baptize, and teach the gospel. Church leaders asked, "How do we 'go into the world' of Comanche, Oklahoma?" In response, church leaders started a free breakfast program on the last Saturday of each month, placing newspaper ads and posting signs that read, "Free Breakfast." After a few months, they drew fifty or sixty persons. After this, the breakfast committee decided to remove the word "free" and simply call it a "community breakfast." Younger families who came to breakfast had told them they felt singled out as persons who needed a handout. After the name change, attendance grew to 125. The church had moved from study to action.[9]

Study can be incorporated into an overall strategy of leadership development for low-income persons. Circles USA relies on a combination of personal goal setting and group support to lift the poor out of poverty. Participants offer a twelve-week class for those living in poverty called "Getting Ahead," which combines personal financial management with lessons about social causes of poverty. Upon graduation, participants make a commitment, usually for eighteen months to five years, to get out of poverty permanently. The graduate, now known as a "Circle Leader," is assigned a person known as an Ally. "Allies are not mentors. They are intentional friends," according to Rebecca Lewis, the Circles Coach at First United Methodist Church in McPherson, Kansas. Participants are invited to attend monthly training

9. Jeanne Stevenson-Moessner, *Prelude to Practical Theology* (Nashville: Abingdon, 2008), 13–17.

sessions alongside others who are committed to similar goals. This group-centered approach makes the task of study so much more enjoyable than it would be in isolation.[10]

To the more actively oriented, study may seem like a classic waste of time. Its benefits may be intangible yet long lasting, opening up new visions for what needs to be done, serving as a catalyst to action, and making it more likely that the action we do undertake will achieve its desired effect.

10. "Dots Start to Connect," YouTube video, 6:00, uploaded September 21, 206 by Dana Horrell, https://tinyurl.com/yaulc2s4.

8

Enlist Specialists

Expert knowledge can be invaluable. Specialists can help to navigate a complicated world filled with systems and technologies that require professional knowledge. If used rightly, their knowledge can deepen our understanding of patterns that shape our lives.

Church leaders can greatly benefit from the use of social workers and other specialists, such as economists, city planners, and rural sociologists. Paul Lichterman studied another group of church leaders that shows how it can be done. The Park Cluster, a group of a dozen white volunteers from affluent neighborhoods, ventured three miles away to the Park community, a low-income neighborhood of mostly African American, Hmong, Vietnamese, and Spanish-speaking Central Americans.[1] Each month the group drove over to "help out" and "build community." When they approached the

1. Paul Lichterman, *Elusive Togetherness: Church Groups Trying to Bridge America's Divisions* (Princeton: Princeton University Press, 2005), 171–215.

director of the local neighborhood center to ask what they could do, she recruited Kendra, a social worker who knew the neighborhood well. For Kendra, the Cluster represented a pool of volunteers who could be plugged into short-term assignments—setting up party tables, picking up food donations from grocery stores, collecting donated goods from churches, and repairing shelves in the food pantry. For the volunteers, however, Kendra could provide them much-needed knowledge of the community until they could navigate the culture of the neighborhood on their own.

Initially, Kendra ran everything. Volunteers did not often think for themselves. They did not investigate their own experience. Their monthly meetings were businesslike, with members reporting on the tasks accomplished. Members spoke "mainly to *report* on tasks accomplished or to ask simple questions." Yet over time, the group's operating style began to change. They began spending less time talking about the tasks they accomplished and more about the neighborhoods they were getting to know. Instead of just receiving assignments, they peppered Kendra with questions about why the community was so poor and services so few. They became curious about the institutions that held the community together—the neighborhood center and other helping agencies, the stores, the schools, the banks, the churches. They spoke less about a community in need and more about the neighborhood's remarkable diversity of black, Vietnamese, Hmong, Latino, and white residents.

At times ordinary people become so skeptical of expert

knowledge that they insist on flying by their own misguided lights to the harm of the community they are trying to help. Frank Fischer, a political scientist, points out that conflict between citizens and experts seems to be the order the day. In many issues of public concern, decision-making "more and more becomes a struggle between those who have expertise and those who do not." He argues that we need "to put the relationship of citizens and experts together in a new way."[2]

The Park Cluster volunteers demonstrate this new way of using specialists. Instead of relying solely on Kendra's expertise, they developed their own "social map" of the community. Ned talked about all the different thrift shops, and Mary knew all about the local elementary schools and could tell the group which ones had nearby congregations and synagogues that might be approached in the future to sponsor tutoring programs. They used Kendra as their resource instead of letting her do all the thinking.

The case of Adopt-A-Family shows what can go wrong when we fail to enlist specialists. Paul Lichterman, a sociologist, studied this faith-based program, whose purpose was to target African American families in order to "pull them" out of poverty. Sponsored by a cluster of evangelical churches, the program intended to improve the lives of low-income families by building strong ties to middle-class volunteers from churches in the area. Adopt-A-Family centered its model on the concept of "Christ-like care." In this model,

2. Frank Fischer, *Citizens, Experts, and the Environment: The Politics of Local Knowledge* (Durham, NC: Duke University Press, 2000), 8, 23.

specialists would not be required and would only hamper the operation of Christian love. At their orientation, Teri, the keynote speaker, explained this approach. Lichterman summarizes her remarks. "Each individual was a gift to behold. To remark on adopted families' social backgrounds, to note that the families were mostly black, that they lived in poor neighborhoods, would only bring up 'cultural barriers.' That would be negative. Teri knew about cultural differences, she assured us, and had spoken about them to other audiences, but that was not why she was here tonight. 'I'm not going to do a cultural thing. I'm going to speak from what I know from God.' What she knew with quiet certainty was that each individual was special and deserved to be treated as one would serve God."[3] For Teri, dwelling on social or cultural differences detracted from the idea that we are all made in the image of God. Volunteers would not need the cultural, social, or economic knowledge that experts provide. Instead, they would focus on what everyone—whites and blacks, rich and poor—held in common.

The decision not to use specialists hampered the effectiveness of the Adopt-A-Family program. One group's experience illustrates the point. Community in Christ Church adopted a family headed by Quenora, a young single mother, but within six months they terminated their relationship. Quenora's behavior frustrated and puzzled them. In their first activity, two volunteers, Pat and Kara, took Quenora to a doctor's appointment. Afterward, they offered to take her out

3. Lichterman, *Elusive Togetherness*, 133–34.

for a snow cone. But here was the surprise: instead of taking them to an ice cream shop, they stopped at a street vendor's cart instead. Kara told her pastor, "This is where she lives! This is what she's about. . . . My immediate reaction was 'I want to move her out of here!' That's my long-term prayer." Pastor Nick remarked, "It sounds like you had some culture shock." A social worker with expertise and deep knowledge of the neighborhood might have helped Kara gain a better appreciation for Quenora's neighborhood.

Yet the group never sought a social worker's help. Instead, they talked with themselves endlessly about what made Quenora tick. Why did she need rides from us to everywhere? Why did she not ride the buses? Why was she not always home after she had promised to be there? Why was she so often hard to contact? Without a specialist, the group was left to figure it out on their own. After six months, the group decided to terminate the relationship, citing Quenora's apparent unwillingness to partner with them. The social worker's expertise might have helped them understand a young mother's situation.[4]

Church leaders have more power than we realize to use specialists to serve our agendas rather than relinquishing our authority to make decisions. The Park Cluster provides a case in point. More experts are practicing "advocacy research" that puts their expertise at the service of ordinary citizens. In this model, the expert does not provide technical answers but acts

4. Lichterman, *Elusive Togetherness*, 133–70, 141.

more as a "facilitator of public learning and empowerment." Here the expert assumes the role of "specialized citizen."[5]

Despite the potential for misuse, experts can offer judgments that prove to be pivotal for church leaders trying to navigate a complicated social situation. In many cases, these individuals have spent years researching the social, cultural, and economic systems that influence the communities we serve. We should enlist their help whenever possible.

5. Fischer, *Citizens, Experts, and the Environment*, 37, 40.

9

Pose Questions about Your Experience

Confronted with a perplexing situation, pose questions about your experience. Ask early and often. Challenging our own understanding with questions enables us to dive below the surface and uncover what may not seem obvious at first.

Taking the time to probe the situation can be frustrating for some people. Ned expressed his frustration with the Park Cluster, the group of volunteers who drove in monthly to a low-income neighborhood to volunteer (see previous chapter). Early in the group's life, it spent meetings reporting on its tasks to Kendra, but as time went on, the group's conversations got lengthier as they questioned their work and delved into ways to bring lasting change to the community. Confronted with the many health needs in the community, the group eventually made the decision to hire a parish nurse. This decision led to ongoing and sometimes complicated discussions about the project. In Ned's view, the group's new direction distracted from the real work that needed to be done. At one meeting, he told the group, "My vision in the early days was a couple of people coming and meeting and helpin' out. And now it's become way too mechanical." For Ned, discussions had gotten too complicated. "At this point, I'd just as soon step back and let the center tell me what it needs. I question the need for this group."[1] For Ned, the needs were obvious, and asking questions merely slowed things down.

Posing questions can help us to uncover hidden problems, dynamics, and potential in our community projects. Ann Morisy, a lay theologian based in London, tells of visiting a church-run thrift shop located in a mining community in the countryside. Leaders had been frustrated by the lack of volunteers involved in the program, particularly men. They invited Morisy to review the situation. She began by posing a series of questions. "What is the most important thing about the shop?" she asked. Almost everyone answered: being able to sit around the fireplace and talk. People would sit by the fire and talk about politics or exchange the latest in local gossip. Next Morisy asked, "What is it about the fire that is so important?" Some answered that it brought back happy memories of sitting around the fire at home enjoying conversation with family and friends. Why did that not happen now? They answered that many people had left town, leav-

1. Paul Lichterman, *Elusive Togetherness: Church Groups Trying to Bridge America's Divisions* (Princeton: Princeton University Press, 2005), 194.

ing the old timers behind. Then she asked, "Who lights the fire each morning?" and "Who stokes the fire?" It turned out the men took care of this. She asked why it was the men who took responsibility for the fire. At this point, Morisy recounts the response she received: "Because that's all they're good for," came the half-mocking response from the women in the group. Why is it that this is all the men are good for? From here the discussion came alive; it was no longer a quaint insight into the mores of a mining community. The discussion took full account of the pit closures and the sense of uselessness the men felt. The truth was that the town had entered decline, and many talented young people had left, with only the old or the "good for nothings" (in their own words) remaining. The men then offered their opinion about the thrift shop run by the church: it did not really help matters. What man would want to fold clothes and arrange used items on shelves for sale?

These probing questions had laid the situation bare for all to see. In response, the shop decided to change its focus. They would take over a warehouse and set up a café for the community. This new arrangement provided jobs for both men and women to do, such as driving to the store with vans filled with clothing and furniture when homes needed to be vacated, but also restoring furniture, delivering furniture to families in need, and sorting goods for sale. Morisey observes, "The church saw that the emphasis on recycling was not limited to material goods; it was people who were being salvaged as well."[2] The new direction began with a series of probing questions.

The "problem probe" represents one technique enabling groups to understand the full dimensions of a given problem. This method can be especially helpful when the problem has a history of unsuccessful attempts to solve it. The problem probe offers a structured set of questions to uncover the full dimension of the problem being confronted. To begin the probe, ask each group member to write down what they think the problem is, using a word, sentence, or even a brief paragraph. Then lead the group through a series of probing questions, usually no more than eight, to draw out the nature of the problem. Examples of probing questions include: What happens? Then what happens? Where does the problem occur? When does the problem occur? How frequently does it occur? Who is most affected by the problem? When was the problem first identified as being a significant problem? Is this problem much like other problems that have occurred in the past? If yes, does there appear to be a pattern operating here? How did things work before we had this problem?[3]

As they answer, encourage to people to use "I" statements to convey their personal point of view and to be as objective as possible when describing the problem. Problem probing allows you to get a better understanding of the full dimensions of the challenge you face. Clarifying the nature of the

2. Ann Morisy, *Beyond the Good Samaritan* (London: Bloomsbury, 1997), 77–78.
3. Thomas Justice and David W. Jamieson, *The Facilitator's Handbook* (New York: HRD, 1999).

problem may be a first step toward reaching consensus on a possible solution.[4]

Reflecting on experience can only get you so far. Action still matters. In the parable of the last judgment in Matthew 25, the Son of Man blesses the servant for taking good actions, not thinking good thoughts: "For I was hungry and you gave me food, I was thirsty and you gave me something to drink, I was a stranger and you welcomed me, I was naked and you gave me clothing, I was sick and you took care of me, I was in prison and you visited me" (Matthew 25:34–36). Good action requires rolling up the sleeves and getting to work. Yet each one of these actions—feeding, offering drink, clothing, caregiving, and visiting—has a relational dimension as well. Relationships are built on conversation, give and take, and question and answer. Like the other reflective tools in this section, posing questions and answering them gets us into the kind of action that builds relationships and strengthens community.

4. Justice and Jamieson, *Facilitator's Handbook*, 169–71.

10

Write It Up

It may seem strange to include *writing* among a list of tools for community engagement. Typically seen as a solitary activity, writing may seem like the opposite of active engagement. Yet writing allows us to reflect in a way that could benefit even the most hands-on activist. Many churches would benefit from less doing and more writing it up.

Writing can be used after a mission trip. Ten years after the event, Dee Ann reflected back on her time as a student on a travel and study seminar to Central America sponsored by the Presbyterian Church (USA). She described a feeling of "danger and cautiousness" in visiting Guatemala, El Salvador, and Nicaragua during the El Salvador civil war and recounted visits with business, church, and social-justice leaders that gave her "new eyes, new heart, new view of life." "Through many of the people we met . . . we experienced a level of faith that before had been unimaginable." Writing can be used not only to recollect but also to maintain a real-time record of events. Some mission teams keep a group journal, asking a different person each day to record the group's experience from their perspective. The resulting account can be copied at the end of the trip and shared with everyone, or excerpts can be used for articles and presentations about the trip.[1]

Whether kept by individuals or groups, journals come in all stripes. Your journal could be a record of the facts of the case: Who? What? When? Where? It could consist of short notes to aid memory or gather ideas to think about later, or it might include detailed descriptions in case you want to write about it later. It could contain something more personal, such as stories you hear or observations you make. It might capture a reflective piece focused more on your inner thoughts, memories, and feelings rather than the experience itself. Some writers use the journal as a place to dump negative feelings about their experience so that these feelings can be set aside for the time being and reviewed later when the writer is feeling calmer and more collected. For the more analytical types, the journal could be used for theological or ethical analysis about the situations they encounter.[2]

Some outreach teams find that a mission statement helps clarify purpose. Describing briefly why your team exists will help you to focus on what's really important. The process of forging a mission statement enables the group to achieve a shared understanding. For that reason, be sure to include

1. Debby Vial, *When God's People Travel Together* (Louisville: Presbyterian Peacemaking Program, 1999), 46, 54.
2. Jean McNiff, Pamela Lomax, and Jack Whitehead, *You and Your Action Research Project* (New York: Routledge, 1997), 87–88.

time for discussion and debate before writing it down. Before beginning the process, instruct the group in this way: "When we craft a mission statement, the statement is more than words. It represents the debate and discussion we've gone through to write it. It gets pulled out and used regularly. It helps us make good decisions."

The revision process helps to focus on your broad intentions rather than on wordsmithing. The end result should be a brief, clear, inspiring statement describing why you exist. Read it aloud at meetings, and spend a few minutes discussing key words or sharing stories about how you fulfilled it. A large Presbyterian women's group worked hard on a shared statement at a women's retreat. Three months later, the group was approached by the senior pastor with a request for the group to take on a new task. After spending about one minute reviewing their mission statement, the members decided the project was not in alignment with it. The pastor was impressed with their focus. The statement made it easy to decide what action to take.[3]

A memo of understanding (MOU) functions somewhat like a mission statement, though its focus is more external. The MOU serves to clarify how your team will collaborate with others, ensuring that your partners, including donors, expert advisors, social-service agencies, and even the program's beneficiaries, are all on the same page. A typical MOU creates a blueprint for action that states the goal of the pro-

3. Susan Waechter and Deborah Kocsis, *How to Energize Your Volunteer Ministry* (Loveland, CO: Group, 2004), 37, 42–43, 104.

gram, the activities to be carried out, and what is expected of each partner. How will differences be resolved? Will a pastor or wise elder be consulted, or will you appoint an arbitration team consisting of representatives of each partner group?

The final product could be brief, usually no more than one or two pages long. Not a legal document, the MOU simply ensures understanding by everyone involved. For example, a church mission team wants to develop a community garden in order to supply the neighborhood with fresh produce. Partners might include volunteers supplied by the church or community, expert gardeners from the local garden club, and city officials who give approval. A well-written MOU could ensure that the partners do not work at cross purposes due to misunderstanding.[4]

A program history, written to keep track of actions taken over time, offers another writing tool for ministry teams. Christ Lutheran Church in Whitefish, Montana, created a program history after it developed Shepherd's Hand Clinic, a free medical clinic for people unable to afford health care. As the ministry began to expand, its leaders felt compelled to keep track. They decided to document their steps in a simple record of what steps were taken when. This running history gave the leadership an idea of the amount of time needed for each step and allowed them to look back and evaluate how they met their initial goals or fell short.[5]

Everyone should be invited to write, including the low-

4. Sandra Swan, *The New Outreach* (New York: Church Publishing, 2010), 156–57.
5. Linda-Marie Delloff, *Public Offerings: Stories from the Front Lines of Community Ministry* (Bethesda, MD: Alban Institute), 73.

income residents that so many churches serve. Brown Memorial United Methodist Church in Syracuse, New York, offered writing exercises for customers at its food pantry. Located on the city's impoverished Near West Side, the church serves as a community center for the neighborhood. After shopping at the pantry, residents were invited to sit at a table in the corridor where people lined up to enter. Writers were offered printed sheets with a writing prompt (a question or brief description to respond to) at the top of a page, which was otherwise blank. One topic was sidewalks, with the prompt: "Do you use the sidewalk? What do you think of the sidewalks?" Non-English speakers were offered prompts in Spanish, with the account to be translated into English later. Those who could not write could draw a picture, and others chose to both write and draw pictures. Used initially as an organizing tool for resident groups to seek action from the city council, these writings were also published in a small, inexpensive paperback, *West Side Walks*. The program's director, Steve Parks, associate professor of writing at Syracuse University, got the idea from the Federation of Worker Writers and Community Publishers in the United Kingdom, a thirty-year-old network of community writing groups. "Our mission is to provide opportunities for local communities to represent themselves by telling their stories in their own words."[6] Church leaders wanting to empower the neighbors they serve should consider asking them to write.

Writing belongs to everyone. For some people, writing

6. New City Community Press, www.newcitycommunitypress.com.

may seem to be a difficult, unpleasant, and nearly impossible task. For others, it can be exhilarating, satisfying, and self-revelatory. Everyone should have the opportunity to try it. This tool has been underutilized.

11

Cultivate Self-Awareness

"First do no harm" applies equally well to medicine and community engagement. Though we may act with the best of intentions, the law of unintended consequences still applies, and it can bring harm if we are not careful. Cultivating self-awareness may reduce the potential for damage. Watch for hidden attitudes and subliminal messages when offering help. A little awareness can go a long way.

Robert Lupton addresses the importance of cultivating self-awareness in his book *Toxic Charity*. He advises church volunteers to become aware of "subliminal attitudes and messages" conveyed when offering volunteer help. He recommends asking local residents to help you whenever going into a community, especially if you are not yet familiar with that particular community. Encourage the residents to get organized, assess their own needs, identify resources in the community, and then determine whether outside help is actually needed. Once you enter the community to work, find ways to get to know residents through holding conversations during lunch, at someone's place of employment, or in people's homes. Such conversations can raise your own awareness of local attitudes.[1]

Mission trips overseas can be just as laden with misjudgment as domestic work trips. Consider this fictional example inspired by real experiences. Moments after the ten-passenger van arrives in the Central American village of San Valente, Jenna pulls out her camera to photograph the dozens of patchwork buildings made of corrugated metal, plastic, and wood. Scott, the trip's coordinator, asks the group to help hand out the goods, which will arrive via truck that afternoon, to community residents. This mission trip's purpose is to lay the foundation for a new community church. The mission-trip leader sent money in advance to hire someone to dig the foundation trenches. However, when the group arrives at the work site, they are shocked because the trenches are only half-finished. Miguel, their host, explains the reason: they prefer to hire local workers with hand tools, not a single person with heavy machinery, so that more people can be employed. "Looks like it's going to be a long week!" Jenna exclaims.

How could these missioners cultivate more self-awareness? Before Jenna reaches for her camera, she and her friends could get to know their hosts and gain an understanding of what it is like to live there. Otherwise, the trip—whether to El

1. Robert Lupton, *Toxic Charity: How Churches and Charities Hurt Those They Help (and How to Reverse It)* (New York: HarperCollins, 2013), 150–51.

Salvador or inner-city Detroit—becomes voyeuristic or like a tourist destination. Scott, the trip leader, might want to reconsider his plan to hand out supplies from the back of a pickup truck. This can be an offensive practice, as it reinforces a pattern of top-down paternalism. Instead, Scott could consider giving the items to a local service agency or congregation to distribute. Jenna, who expressed shock over a half-finished trench, needs to respect that she and her group have now entered their hosts' world. Logistics and timelines need to proceed under local direction.[2]

Despite their potential for harm, mission trips can also open us to the possibility of cultivating a whole new awareness. Travel, especially to the Global South, can cause us to question established thinking. Lauri Occhipinti, a cultural anthropologist, observed how overseas travel can "crack open" the cultural assumptions of church mission volunteers. She joined a weeklong mission trip sponsored by New Wilmington Presbyterian Church in western Pennsylvania as a participant observer, traveling to the city of Sabaneta, Dominican Republic.

Occhipinti discovered that people who embarked on mission trips in order to "help people in need" or "learn about problems in other parts of the world" often returned with a whole new outlook on the place they were trying to help. Central to their new attitude was a critique of the excesses of their own American culture—including consumerism,

2. This writing appeared in my article, "Short-Term Mission Trips Yield Long-Term Success," *The Parish Paper* 25, no. 10 (October 2017).

careerism, and American exceptionalism. Immersion in a new culture aroused questions about once tried-and-true values.

Cultural exchanges can work that way. These American missioners returned from their experience more aware of how spoiled Americans can become by their material wealth. One health-care provider described what it was like to return to the United States: "All last week, I felt depressed. It was hard to readjust. People are so spoiled in our health-care system. People kept coming in and complaining about little things. I compare that to what we saw in poor neighborhoods around Sabaneta." These missioners also learned that life does not always have to be fast-paced. Members of the Sabaneta team saw that people in the Dominican Republic spent time on the street and on their front porches, talking with neighbors. They also learned that Americans tend to value possessions more than relationships. One minister, who had been on many mission trips, said, "It is easy for Americans to be distracted by a whole lot of junk. . . . In other places, there's not as much junk—I don't know how to say what I am getting at. It helps me to see what is extraneous in my life, and what is central. In the Dominican, we see people's relationships with one another. That is what they focus on. A lot of the things that we do are not so relationship based."[3]

To cultivate self-awareness among your volunteers, whether here or abroad, find a time and place for the group to reflect on their experience afterward. Orientation and

3. Laurie Occhipinti, *Making a Difference in a Globalized World: Short-term Missions That Work* (Lanham, MD: Rowman & Littlefield, 2014), 34–38.

debriefing sessions offer an opportunity for workers to cultivate self-awareness in a psychologically safe group setting. Everyone should be encouraged to provide input. Self-awareness can not only prevent damage in others but foster growth in ourselves.

PART III

Mapping Tools

12

Do a Survey

If you need to get basic data about a large group of people (say, more than thirty), a simple survey might do the trick. It need not be elaborate. A paper and pencil survey, administered in person, might be sufficient in many cases.

Surveys are questionnaires designed to provide relevant facts about a group that you care about and perhaps work with every day. Surveys can provide basic facts about the customers who use your program or service, or they may help you get a sense of what they think about different options to improve it.[1] Before designing a survey, first try to determine whether you can get the information using another method. For instance, web-based demographic services such as Mission Insite can provide congregations with demographic information about the community without the need for a

1. Tina Nabatchi and Matt Leighninger, *Public Participation for the 21st Century* (Hoboken, NJ: Jossey-Bass, 2015), 217.

survey. However, if you have more particular questions you want answered, a survey may be just the thing.

Surveys can be done by phone, email, or in person. In recent years, online platforms such as Survey Monkey, Survey Console, or Survey Gizmo can provide services for email surveys and also provide assistance in designing your own survey. Survey Monkey provides extensive resources for online surveys, including how to design a survey, how to get people to respond, and how to evaluate your responses. Consult them or ask an expert before designing your survey.

The following suggestions may help you get started in designing a survey. (1) See whether someone else has already gathered the information you need in order to determine whether a survey is needed and what should be asked. (2) Talk to persons who already have strong opinions about your topic and who can help you shape your questions. (3) Get advice from a polling expert or visit an online polling platform to get help in writing the questions. (4) Do a focus group or talk one on one with several persons to get a better sense of what to ask. (5) Determine how you will get the information to your respondents—in person, by phone, or by email. (6) Select your target audience, and find ways to sample this group so that your results are representative. (7) Do a pilot survey to test the questions.[2]

When designing the survey, be sure to group similar questions so that the survey is easy to follow. Ask the same ques-

2. "Survey," The National Coalition for Dialogue and Deliberation, http://ncdd.org/rc/item/1559/.

tion in a series of surveys in order to build a baseline. Keep the survey as short as possible, and ease into it by making your first question easy to answer, saving difficult or sensitive questions for later. Be specific and explore only one idea at a time, clarifying anything that could be interpreted in multiple ways. Ask only questions that are relevant to what you want to know, and avoid yes and no questions, which often fail to capture nuances in people's views. Avoid using a matrix, a survey design that requires people to focus on multiple questions at once. Use words, not numbers, in designing answer choices. For instance, "slightly likely" or "extremely likely" are better than numbers like two and four to indicate preference.[3]

How do you determine who to survey? If you want to survey the entire population and the group is 250 or fewer, then hand out the survey to everyone. If the group is larger, you may want to sample, or select from, the entire population. If so, then each person should theoretically have an equal chance to get the form. One idea: flip a coin or toss a die to choose where to begin on your list, and then select every second, third, or fourth person until you have reached the end. Alternatively, you could do what is known as a stratified sample. Subdivide the group into distinct subgroups (for example, by age, race, where they live, how long they have been using the program or service) and then select persons from

3. "The Nuts and Bolts of Creating Surveys," SurveyMonkey, https://tinyurl.com/y7f4f7bg.

each subgroup using a method that allows you to randomize. This method works well with a highly diverse population.

What you want to avoid at all costs is what is referred to as an "accidental sample." For instance, you might choose to survey whatever group happens to be at hand, such as the next twenty people who walk through the door or a group that gathers at a particular location each day. While the selection may seem random, it can be impossible to tell whether the group has gathered randomly or has a specific reason for being where they are at the moment. In this case, they constitute a distinct subgroup and not a sample representative of the whole population.[4]

We are all familiar with surveys. Who hasn't been invited to take a survey after joining an online community, purchasing a product, or visiting the doctor? Yet familiarity with this tool might cause it to be easily overlooked. A narrowly focused survey designed around your own questions may provide just enough information about your group or project to avoid costly mistakes or misunderstandings.

4. Scott Thumma, "Methods for Congregational Study," in *Studying Congregations: A New Handbook*, ed. Nancy Ammerman et al. (Nashville: Abingdon, 1998), 218–20.

13

Hold a Focus Group

Listening works for political officials seeking to act on behalf of their constituents, and it works equally well for church leaders seeking to engage the community. A focus group represents one tool for listening to the community. Simple in design, it honors the experience of our neighbors in the stories they tell, the questions they ask, and the concerns they express.

A focus group typically consists of eight to ten participants who meet for ninety minutes to two hours of discussion led by a trained moderator. Another key factor that makes it a focus group is the narrow range of persons invited to contribute. In order to facilitate discussion, plan to invite people who share a common demographic (such as age, race, or income) or similar interests or relationship to the topic at hand. For instance, if you want to learn more about your food-pantry program, do not include both volunteers and customers in the same focus group.[1]

As a group listening process, focus groups inhabit their own niche within the range of engagement tools. Unlike a planning meeting, the purpose here is not to generate ideas for future action or forge agreement about a strategic plan. Instead, the goal is to uncover attitudes or opinions that may lie hidden beneath the surface. At the same time, a focus group differs from a one-on-one conversation (see "Hold a One-on-One Interview," chap. 21) in that it builds on the synergy that emerges as group members respond to what others are saying.

A good moderator is key to focus-group success. Does this mean you should hire someone from outside? Not necessarily. If cost is a factor, then ask an insider, such as a pastor or the program director, to conduct the focus group. In either case, seek someone who prepares well, knows the basics of group dynamics, and is committed to fairness. One argument in favor of conducting your own focus group is the benefit of knowing more than any outsider would about the program or service being evaluated. On the other hand, an experienced moderator can bring an expertise in focus-group method, which is more important than technical knowledge of the topic under discussion. Beyond this, an outside moderator can be expected to have no particular investment in the outcome of the discussion, which increases the likelihood of getting an unbiased interpretation of the situation. On the other hand, there is no reason that a self-aware insider, some-

1. Thomas L. Greenbaum, *The Handbook for Focus Group Research*, 2nd ed. (Thousand Oaks, CA: Sage, 1998), 2.

one committed to fairness in group process, could not get the job done adequately and for a fraction of the cost of hiring an outsider.[2] So it depends on your situation.

Whether insider or outsider, a good moderator must have the ability to listen well, paying attention to what is said and paraphrasing or restating the participant's comments when necessary to reflect that they have been heard. The moderator must have an excellent short-term auditory memory, remembering comments made early in the group and correlating them later with comments made by the same participants. Finally, the best moderators know how to establish a rapport with group members in a short time and think on their feet, using the information the group generates to determine the best line of questioning later.[3]

If you yourself serve as the moderator, plan to prepare a discussion guide ahead of time. Questions must be mapped out in advance yet kept open ended so that the conversation can go in any number of directions. Move from the general to the specific in asking questions, and record answers on a flip chart or have someone take notes.

To organize a focus group, first define the problem or research question, and then write a statement of the group's purpose. For example, "This focus group will explore ways to better serve the needs of our food-pantry customers by understanding their experience in coming to us."

Next you will need to identify a sampling frame (who

2. Greenbaum, *Handbook for Focus Group Research*, 68–69.
3. Greenbaum, *Handbook for Focus Group Research*, 77–79.

are your participants?) and identify a moderator. Next invite your participants. Consider including small incentives to attend, such as stipends, childcare, meals, or snacks. It doesn't hurt to overbook by at least 10 percent.

Once you have gathered the focus group, welcome the participants, briefly state the purpose of the group, and break the ice by having people introduce themselves and their experience with the issue. One idea would be to have each one tell a story related to the question under discussion. Next, let people know what questions will be asked and what you will do with the data. At this point, introduce a few ground rules for discussion.

If you are unclear about how to start, you might try asking a fairly general question that anyone can respond to, and ask each person to share. As moderator, make sure everyone participates. You can accomplish this by having group members reply either in random or specific order. It is ideal if everyone responds to each question, but you may also need to allow someone to pass. Another trick to ensure that people are selected randomly is to use a pack of three-by-five cards with names on them, pull the names of two or three persons, and ask them to respond.

How you evaluate the data depends on how you recorded it. If you recorded the entire session either with audio or video, you could transcribe it word for word and analyze the transcription. You may need the permission of all the participants to record the group. This is especially true for video recording. If you are taking notes, analyze them. Some people might prefer to work entirely from memory, but this only works if you debrief with a group immediately after it is over and ask their help with analysis. Analyzing involves looking for themes in the material (sometimes called "coding"). What material? It could be the words people use, the frequency of certain answers to questions, the intensity of the responses, or how specific the answers. The more closely tied an answer to a specific experience, the better.

Now you are ready to write a report.[4] Focus groups offer a great chance to hear from people and strengthen community at the same time. Group interviews allow people to build off the ideas of others in the group, respond emotionally to powerful stories told by others, and offer insights that emerge from the process of sharing with others. Still, focus groups have their limitations. For one thing, the answers you receive will only be as good as the questions asked and the process of selecting your group. Also, unlike a professionally administered survey using a random sample (quantitative research), a focus group will yield insights into how people think and act, but this cannot tell you exactly how many people in your community feel a certain way about your subject. In fact, if done poorly, a focus group could serve to spread gossip and speculation rather than provide solid information. To check and substantiate what you hear in a focus group, try holding multiple interviews with diverse groups in your community.[5]

4. Thomas Justice and David Jamieson, *The Facilitator's Fieldbook* (New York: American Management Association, 1999), 201–10.

5. Scott Thumma, "Methods for Congregational Study," in *Studying Congregations: A New Handbook*, ed. Nancy Ammerman et al. (Nashville: Abingdon, 1998), 208.

Focus groups can be a powerful tool for mapping the community by uncovering the feelings, stories, and opinions of the people around us. The power of this method lies in its ability to use the safety and protection of the group to bring private thoughts into the open. Listening to others about an issue of vital public importance might just be the first step toward change.

14

Map Your Community Together

What better way to get to know the neighborhood than to map it together? That's the idea behind collaborative mapping, a new strategy born out of the rise of computers, the global positioning system (GPS), and digital mapping, which together have replaced physical maps for so many uses. Mapping need not be high tech, however, to be both collaborative and effective. Developing a visual picture of your community and its resources lies at the heart of the mapping enterprise, and pictures can be drawn with pencil and paper and through good, old-fashioned conversation.

Consider employing a mapping exercise at the outset of your community project. Start by defining your community's physical boundaries, including major streets, highways, railroad tracks, or natural boundaries such as hills, valleys, and rivers. Next look for anchor institutions, such as schools, hospitals, prisons, military facilities, or recreational facilities, that provide the basic sources of power and decision-making in the community and provide stability in moments of crisis. Finally, include gathering places, such as churches, parks, schools, service clubs, restaurants, taverns, and street corners.

The community's people constitute a significant part of this analysis. To help you in this process, identify and gather a group to tell stories about the community. Include visual observations of the community by taking a quick drive or walk through the neighborhood (see "Conduct a Community Tour," chap. 15), deliberately looking for the "invisible" people who are marginalized and powerless. Finally, consider intangible forces, such as laws, cultural values, employment patterns, and job security.[1]

Low-tech mapping can be informal and conversational. Paul Lichterman observed how a group of church volunteers used an informal mapping process to get to know the low-income neighborhood they served. The Park Cluster (see "Enlist Specialists," chap. 8, and "Pose Questions about Your Experience," chap. 9) commuted monthly from their tree-lined suburban neighborhoods to the Park neighborhood, a multiethnic, low-income community. Receiving volunteer assignments from a community social worker, the group initially focused on getting their tasks accomplished. As they became more curious about neighborhood institutions, such as the stores, the schools, the banks, and the churches, they

1. Carl S. Dudley, *Community Ministry: New Challenges, Proven Steps to Faith-Based Initiatives* (Bethesda, MD: Alban Institute, 2002), 22–50.

began an informal process that the researcher labelled "social mapping." Ned talked about all the different thrift shops, and Mary knew all about the local elementary schools and could tell the group which ones had congregations and synagogues nearby that might be approached in the future to sponsor tutoring programs. Through their conversations, they carried around in their heads a shared mental map of the neighborhood, its resources, and its problems.[2]

The recent emergence of wiki-platforms such as OpenStreetMap (OSM) (OpenStreetMap.org) offers a place where people with different skills and perspectives can contribute to a single map with features of their community, from assets such as grocery stores, banks, and thrift shops to hazards such as unshoveled sidewalks, reported crime incidents, and potholes. For church leaders willing to engage the newer forms of technology, wiki-platforms offer churches a powerful community-planning tool.[3]

Though mapping has been around since ancient times, digital maps designed for computer or mobile devices greatly increase flexibility. Computer maps are called geographic information systems (GIS), defined as "a computer system for capturing, storing, checking, and displaying data related to positions on Earth's surface."[4] For example, Google Maps starts with a basemap, which consists not of a large, single

2. Paul Lichterman, *Elusive Togetherness: Church Groups Trying to Bridge America's Divisions* (Princeton: Princeton University Press, 2005), 179.
3. Tina Nabatchi and Matt Leighninger, *Public Participation for 21st-Century Democracy* (Hoboken, NJ: Jossey-Bass, 2015), 272–73.
4. "GIS: Geographic Information System," NationalGeographic.org, June 21, 2017, https://tinyurl.com/y9myqwju.

map but a whole lot of tile web maps joined together, and then it layers other images, such as place names, addresses, and even locations of favorite restaurants, on top of this background.

Wiki-platforms such as OpenStreetMap represent an open-source version of Google Maps, and they are free for anyone to use or modify. Now users can create overlays to the basemap provided by OpenStreetMaps, plugging in information they find useful for themselves. OSM operates in a manner comparable to Wikipedia, an encyclopedia whose contributors write and edit articles, subject to the review of other contributors who are part of the community. OSM applies the concept of crowdsourcing to mapmaking.

Church leaders could use online maps in at least two ways: for crisis response and for the mapping of communities too poorly resourced to have their own self-designed maps. Mapping proved invaluable to aid workers in crisis response after the 2010 earthquake that devastated Haiti. Given Haiti's poverty, humanitarian aid workers found themselves hampered by a woeful lack of basic geographic data. On most digital maps, only the major roads were visible, and beyond that lay blank space. Here "citizen geographers" from around the world proved invaluable, digging up hard copies of maps and scanning them to develop a basemap for humanitarian aid workers in the field.

Beyond crisis response, churches could work with low-income neighborhoods to develop collaborative maps to benefit residents, something that commercial map providers have so far failed to do. Commercial map makers have shown little interest in mapping the Kibera community of Nairobi, Kenya, a massive and deeply impoverished section of the city, despite the fact that it is home to hundreds of thousands of people. Users of OpenStreetMap created Map Kibera, which now serves as a comprehensive guide to data that matters for residents, such as water points, toilets, clinics, schools, pharmacies, places of worship, and non-governmental organization offices.[5]

If collaborative mapping could work for Kibera, it could make a difference for the resource-starved communities that many US churches serve. Such communities often lack features that middle- and upper-middle-class neighborhoods take for granted, including high-quality schools, jobs that pay a living wage, banks that offer reasonably priced, non-predatory loans, and supermarkets with adequate selection of fresh foods. In order to improve the situation, churches could collaborate with local resident groups to create a map with features such as food banks, thrift shops, transportation points, and grocery stores offering fresh produce. Such data could not only help service providers but also public policy advocates seeking to bring change.

Church leaders hoping to raise awareness of collaborative work might consider sponsoring a "mapping party." Use the event to train volunteers in developing digital maps. Volunteers could learn how to download aerial photos and alter

5. Sterling Quinn, "OpenStreetMap and Its Use as Open Data," https://tinyurl.com/y8l6e2cc.

them using web browser–based editing software. Volunteers who prefer to explore the neighborhood themselves could go out for a walk, a bike ride, or drive around the community using GPS units to mark their location and notepads to write down the information, coming back later to record the data on a computer.

Collaborative mapping requires teamwork but not high-end technology. However, those with a technical bent can use wiki-platforms such as OpenStreetMap to create a specialized, self-generated community map. Whether high tech or not, mapping provides a way for community members to develop a sense of place through visually representing different aspects of the community in relation to its geography. When undertaken with others, mapping provides one more basis for building community.

15

Conduct a Community Tour

Let's take a walk. While it could be done for exercise, most community tours entail something more purposeful. We walk in order to get a better sense of the neighborhood.

What are you looking for? You could be observing housing conditions, infrastructure needs (such as roads and bridges), the presence or absence of businesses, or the types of public space (such as parks and libraries) available. Or you could be observing the people: how many people do you see at a given time of day, and where are they going? What is the traffic like? How is the noise level? Again, the common aspect here is that all of these are things you can observe with your eyes and ears.

A community tour could be helpful in bringing about a shared understanding of the situation faced by the community. Conflict mediators stress the importance of "joint fact finding" to break an impasse and to achieve common understanding. In the same way, when neighbors confront the same set of facts, such as broken sidewalks and stop signs bent out of shape, it makes it easier to do something together about the problems.

Calling it a tour implies something more systematic than simply wandering around the neighborhood to see what can be discovered. For this reason, a checklist will be necessary. What sights do you want to see? What questions do you want answered? If you are doing a windshield tour (by car or bus), it works best to have a team of two in charge—one to drive and the other to guide participants as they observe and record their observations.

For a walking tour, a few guidelines might help. First of all, try to be unobtrusive. When working with a team, this would mean splitting the group up into groups of two or three. A group of five or six constitutes a crowd and could draw attention. Second, try taking part in everyday activities such as taking public transportation, buying something at a store, or eating in a restaurant. Third, take notes as you go along and discuss your observations. Finally, in some cases, you may want to combine walking and driving, particularly when you need to cover a city or a large neighborhood or when safety is a consideration. Some communities were not built for pedestrian traffic and may not be safely walkable.

Later you may want to analyze what you observed. The following questions might be helpful in doing a debriefing or analysis after the tour: What are the community's outstanding assets? What seem to be the community's biggest challenges? What is the most striking thing about the community? What is the most unexpected? What strikes you about the aesthetic quality the community, either positively or negatively?

What might this look in practice? Latino Health for All Coalition took a windshield tour of a predominantly Latino neighborhood in Kansas City, Kansas, to assess the condition of seven different sites for physical activities, such as gyms, pools, and playing fields, in a neighborhood that was approximately one by one-and-a-half miles. In preparation, the leaders did an internet search of facilities, then used free online mapping tools to create a map with the sites on them and to establish the boundaries of the community. They printed maps and drove through the community, stopping and getting out to assess the facilities at each location and using a digital voice recorder and camera to document what they discovered. This tour took about fifteen hours to complete. Afterward the leaders developed a list of physical-activity resources for the community. They asked key stakeholders, such as parents, about their experiences at the sites and how often they used them, which went into the final report.[1]

Tours may be undertaken in response to immediate community needs. In north Philadelphia, for example, a nonprofit organization called Centro Nueva Creacion (New Creation Center) used tours to build self-esteem in the neighborhood's children. Fairhill, a predominantly Latino neighborhood, has for years experienced violence related to drug trafficking and has been nicknamed "The Badlands" by the media for

1. Daniel T. Schober, "Example: A Windshield Tour to Assess Physical Activity Resources in Kansas City," Community Tool Box, https://tinyurl.com/yaqjbabk.

that reason. To counter negative stereotypes, the center calls itself "The Goodlands Project" and uses the arts—yoga, painting, gardening, poetry, and photography—to help children explore the many good things in both the surrounding neighborhood and their own cultural heritage. Once a week, when photography is taught, the children take a tour of the neighborhood, taking pictures of signs of hope they see in their neighborhood. In this way, the children can learn to see their neighborhood in a more positive light than the media portrays.

Touring the neighborhood can be used as a form of intervention. In Los Angeles, the mothers of Dolores Mission Roman Catholic Church undertook a tour to save their community from gang violence. Living in the middle of east Los Angeles, the heart of the gang zone, the mothers felt paralyzed by the presence of thirteen active gangs, each vying for dominance. Killings and injuries happened almost daily. During a particularly violent period, the women began to discuss the crisis in their study group, searching the Scriptures and praying for guidance. One night a woman announced that Jesus had called their study group to do something drastic: they must put aside fear and walk into the heart of the gang's war zone. The group was dumbstruck, but after long discussion, they decided it was time to intervene. Seventy women and a few men began a *peregrinacion*, or pilgrimage, from one gang turf to the next throughout the barrio. Whenever they encountered the young men, they talked with them, offered prayer, and fed them with chips, salsa, and soda. Each night that week, the mothers walked, eventually covering all thirteen war zones. Within a week, gang-related violence plummeted. The mothers formed Comite pro Paz en el Barrio, the Committee for Peace in the Barrio.[2] The intervention, in the form of a community tour, had worked.

Community tours can be undertaken with the broad goal of getting an overview of the neighborhood, or it can be more narrowly focused on one aspect of the community, such as the environment, housing, or street conditions. Whether the scope is broad or narrow, and whether the purpose is observation or intervention, there is no substitute for just doing it. The point is to get out into the community.

2. Ken Butigan, "The Love Walks," *100 Days of Nonviolence*, https://tinyurl.com/y84wymnh.

16

Do Social Analysis

If you want to address systemic issues such as poverty, hunger, and the environment at the local level, some form of social analysis will be required. Social analysis is a method for describing the local community surrounding the church in terms of the social structures that shape it, such as the economic, cultural, and political systems. When done by church leaders, such analysis can help to diagnose the structural reasons for problems, such as poverty or environmental degradation, that they wish to alleviate. On the other hand, social analysis might serve a positive use, uncovering hidden features of the community that can lead to an improved life.[1]

Social analysis may not provide an immediate answer to the question of what action to take, but it can point us in the right direction by providing context within which to work. For example, instead of seeing the poverty experienced by

1. Joe Holland and Peter Henriot, SJ, *Social Analysis: Linking Faith and Justice* (Maryknoll, NY: Orbis, 1983), 103.

low-income working families as an isolated issue, analysis can reveal a larger social fabric that includes the decline of manufacturing in US cities, inadequate health-care policy, and lack of funding for public transportation.

For this reason, social analysis must serve as a necessary first step for church action in the community. Canon Joseph Cardijn (1882–1967), a Belgian Roman Catholic priest who inspired Catholic social-action groups such as the Young Christian Workers, used the phrase "see-judge-act" to provide a framework for action, and the first important step was "seeing." Working with young women, many of them needle workers, prior to World War II, he taught them to start by looking carefully at their work setting and their surrounding relationships rather than looking simply at the facts and figures about a particular situation. Using this "seeing" as first step, they could then "judge" by reflecting on a Christian social teaching that discusses this problem and a Gospel lesson addressing the issue. Then they could "act" by drawing up a plan of action. Borrowing from Cardijn's method, church leaders should analyze their own communities deeply before starting a particular project of neighborhood assistance. Carl Dudley, a church consultant, highlights the importance of surveying the community for the "intangible forces" that influence community life, including local laws, employment patterns, and shared cultural values.[2] To

2. Carl S. Dudley, *Community Ministry: New Challenges, Proven Steps to Faith-Based Initiatives* (Bethesda, MD: Alban Institute), 46–50.

engage in social analysis of your community, move through the following nine steps.[3]

1. *What do you notice about our situation here today?* What are people experiencing? This step is primarily descriptive. We are trying to get a sense of the community without analyzing it too deeply just yet. This description can be done informally by gathering a group and brainstorming, or by asking for stories from people you know. Or it can be accomplished more formally by doing a survey (see pp. 85–88), holding a focus group (see pp. 98–94), conducting a community tour (see pp. 101–5), or holding a series of one-on-one conversations (see pp. 139–345).

2. *What changes have occurred in the past twenty years?* What have been the most important events? This question gets at the historical dimension of the situation. For instance, the New Creation Lutheran Church's decision to launch an after-school program in the late 1990s in the Fairhill neighborhood of north Philadelphia (see "Conduct a Community Tour," chap. 15) was informed by parents' concern about their children's safety after school. Drug trafficking in the neighborhood led to the danger of random violence. A major factor affecting the drug trade was the construction of Interstate 95 decades before, making it easy for dealers to move drugs from north Philadelphia to other cities on the east coast.[4]

3. *What influence does money have in our situation?* This

3. Holland and Henriot, *Social Analysis*, 102.

4. Brian Bennett, "Democrats Aren't the Only Tourists Flocking to Philadelphia. So Are Heroin Addicts," *The Los Angeles Times*, July 23, 2016, https://tinyurl.com/hvznf65.

question addresses the economic system influencing the community. For example, low-income communities tend to have more families struggling with debt due to the prevalence of predatory lending agencies, which is often linked to the decision by banks not locate in such neighborhoods. Furthermore, the economic structure of some of these neighborhoods has deteriorated as middle-income residents have relocated to other neighborhoods.

4. *Who makes the most important decisions around here?* This question addresses the political system, or how power gets exercised. In some cases, the answer can be found by looking at the formal structures that surround us, such as the mayor's office, the city council, the state capital, Congress, or federal agencies. In other cases, we might look to informal structures, such as influential people or families in the community, networks or organizations, or ad hoc coalitions consisting of government and community groups. In one small rural town, the Memorial Day Parade planning committee took on great importance every spring as the holiday approached. For that time period, the planning group exercised an undue influence over town decision-making.

5. *What are the most important relationships people have here?* This question deals with those other social relations so important to nourishing our life together, including the family, the neighborhood, friends at work and school, and social-media connections.

6. *What are the most important traditions of the people?* This addresses the question of culture, including religion, the arts

and music, and local traditions, where we live. In one community, for example, an area-wide barbeque competition serves as an important point of community pride, a chance for people from surrounding towns to socialize with one another, and a chance to learn new tips for the grill. Such traditions shape community life in important ways.

7. *What do people want most in life?* Analyzing a community does not mean simply uncovering its hidden problems, but it also may be used to unearth people's hopes and dreams for the future. Holding a community-wide planning process can be an effective way to bring people together to share their dreams with each other. Appreciative inquiry, a planning method aimed at affirming past strengths and exploring dreams for the future, can help church leaders looking for a positive approach to change.[5]

8. *What will things be like in ten years if they keep going in the same way?* The future focus of this question aims to spark reflection about what is happening in the present. A primary purpose of social analysis is to broaden our perspective to see all the various dimensions of our situation. One planning process that builds directly on this future focus is called the Search Conference. A Search Conference starts with gathering a church or a group of community members together and asking them to extrapolate from current trends if things stay

5. See Mark Lau Branson, *Memories, Hopes, and Conversations: Appreciative Inquiry and Congregational Change*, vol. 1 (Lanham, MD: Rowman & Littlefield, 2004) and Mark Lau Branson, *Memories, Hopes, and Conversations: Appreciative Inquiry, Missional Engagement, and Congregational Change*, vol. 2 (Lanham, MD: Rowman & Littlefield, 2016).

as they are now. The rest of the conference is built around the question, "What is your preferred future?"[6]

9. *What are the most important causes of the way things are today?* This question encourages us to sift through and prioritize among the many causes for a given social reality. For example, hunger continues to be a problem in the United States. According to research done by Bread for the World, a faith-based advocacy group focused on ending hunger, the root cause of hunger is not the lack of food. Worldwide, the primary cause of hunger is poverty. In the United States and other wealthy countries, the primary cause of hunger is poverty resulting from the lack of jobs or the low income generated by most jobs.[7] Based on this social analysis, focusing on job creation or raising the minimum wage might do more to address the root cause of hunger than providing food assistance by itself.

The purpose of social analysis is to describe the multidimensional reality of the communities in which we live. The process can help to shape a direction for our community engagement. Without a grasp of the broader context, our projects can feel like a game of Whac-A-Mole as we seek solutions to local problems in isolation. Additionally, we might miss the positive resources, such as dreams, economic resources, local traditions, and significant relationships, that can help us improve the community in which we live.

6. Merrelyn Emery and Ronald Purser, *The Search Conference: A Powerful Method for Planning Organizational Change and Community Action* (San Francisco: Jossey-Bass, 1996).
7. "What Causes Hunger," Bread for the World, https://tinyurl.com/y8xcuyf9.

PART IV

Dialogue Tools

17

Encourage Team Dialogue

Use conversation and a desire to learn to build a durable team. Team dialogue will enrich the team's service and will likely help sustain the group and keep leaders from burning out. Of course, some may not think of conversation as an important task. In fact, some view conversations as getting in the way of tasks and slowing them down, right? On the contrary, conversation plays an important part in community engagement and must not be ignored. Team talk builds group durability and helps sustain effort. Talking about the work helps to reinforce the reasons for doing what we are doing.

Try this thought experiment: what if we worked less and talked more? Make no mistake: the American volunteer experience is decidedly task-oriented and talk-averse. Sociologist Paul Lichterman observes that a "task-oriented, short-term, plug-in style of volunteering . . . has become nearly synonymous with volunteering in the United States."[1] Churches, like many other non-profit organizations, typically assign volunteers to fill short-term tasks, not long-term assignments. In some ways, the arrangement works out well. Volunteers appreciate that it fits into their busy schedules. With only a few hours commitment, they can experience the satisfaction of having "helped out." It's also easier for staff, who create slots for volunteers to fill and tasks to complete, which can then be quantified and reported to funders. Yet "plug-in" volunteering hampers dialogue.

Working side by side on tasks does not necessarily build a team. Again, Paul Lichterman's research project bears this out. The researcher volunteered for Fun Evenings, a project offering a drug-free, violence-free evening for disadvantaged youth, anticipating many opportunities for conversation. After all, the event had been billed as a "fun evening" at the Downtown Community Center with ping pong, dancing, and youth leadership training provided for the mostly black, Latino, and Laotian teenagers, and a few white teenagers. The volunteers, all white and a generation or two older, would provide supervision.

From the outset, Lichterman found the situation confusing for himself as a volunteer. What exactly was he supposed to be doing? No one else seemed to know either. Polly, the coordinator, had instructed them to monitor the youth and make sure no drugs got in. They were also told that any youth who left should not be allowed back in, though he observed that the volunteers were lax with this requirement.

1. Paul Lichterman, *Elusive Togetherness: Church Groups Trying to Bridge America's Divisions* (Princeton: Princeton University Press, 2005), 66.

Notably lacking was any process for building the team itself. Volunteers exchanged pleasantries and nothing more. "The companionship we strike up is temporary, modular." Unlike other meetings he attended as part of his research, Lichterman observed that he himself was not concerned about how he would come across to others because he knew he would not see these people again. "I gather after two Fun Evenings that we are supposed to be genial with other volunteers but keep our eyes on the scene."[2] "In this particular kids' program," he writes, "being a good volunteer did not necessarily mean developing even temporary relationships with the kids—or talking to them." He observed, "Volunteers sustained loose, easily detachable group bonds with other volunteers. The 'group' in these cases was an aggregate of temporary comrades like Clarisse or Carson with whom one might strike up quick conversations and not see again at the next Fun Evening."[3] Volunteers had been "plugged into" their tasks but not each other. Volunteers had "helped out" but not formed a team. More and deeper talk would have built a stronger team.

Team dialogue can be strengthened in four ways. First, seek to move the team from shallow conversation to a deeper dialogue that airs genuine feelings and brings differences to the surface. Unless it's a Quaker meeting, most small groups have plenty of conversation, yet plentiful talk without real communication can signal trouble. Practicing honesty and

2. Lichterman, *Elusive Togetherness*, 86–87.
3. Lichterman, *Elusive Togetherness*, 88–89.

expecting it from others can strengthen the team and bring to the surface real issues that may need to be dealt with.

One technique for practicing honest conversation is called the EIAG (pronounced eye-ag) process. EIAG is an acronym that stands for Experience, Identify, Analyze, and Generalize. The process allows group members to take a moment to analyze and experience (E), asking what just happened and how it affected every group member. When someone says or does something that could have a big impact on other members, positively or negatively, ask that person, "Would you be willing to explore the effect this had on the others?" If so, ask that person to withhold comments until everyone has finished. Then analyze (A) what happened by asking everyone present to talk about their own reactions. For example, "When [name] said (or did) this, I felt (thought, observed) or I did (or said) this." Or, "When it happened, I assumed this, which led me to react the way I did." After this, you can ask the person whose action you are analyzing, "What was your intention?" Finally, the group can take a moment to generalize (G) or think more broadly about how to act in other situations. Ask the person, "What have you learned?" and ask others the same question. This can deepen the trust required to form a genuine team.[4]

Second, strive for informal, relaxed meetings. The Fun Evenings volunteers never held meetings at all, but simply showed up for their assigned time slots. Regular meetings

4. Jackie Bahn-Henkelman, "Reflection: The Role of the EIAG," *Emotional Intelligence and Human Relations Skills Workshop Student Participant Guide*, EQ-HR: The Center for Emotional Intelligence and Human Relations Skills, 25–27, www.eqhr.org.

empower volunteers to make decisions for themselves, which builds teamwork. Try to avoid "business-like" meetings that can be deadening. Changing the meeting venue from time to time can help keep the conversation fresh. Holding every meeting in "the boardroom" (the designated room where meetings are to take place), can be like always eating in the formal dining room. Look for an informal setting, perhaps somewhere offsite, and share a meal whenever possible to warm up the conversation.

Third, find ways to equalize the conversation so that the same people do not always dominate the conversation. Letting the big talkers have more airtime can be a conversation killer. Granted, some persons are more temperamentally suited to talking and others to listening. Yet the team nearly always gains more from sharing its wisdom than from listening to long-winded monologues. Ask the group to police itself. "If you tend to be a talker, pay attention to how much you talk, and try to talk less. If you tend to be a listener, try to talk more." Or if someone has been quiet, ask, "We have not heard from you yet. What do you think?"[5]

Fourth, draft a team covenant, a written or verbal agreement that describes and defines members' relationships as a team. Lack of trust is a key source of trouble in failing teams. Unless members feel safe and secure with the group, they will not contribute to their full potential. Some groups allow sarcasm to predominate, which stifles those who have sincere

5. Marlene Wilson, *Creating a Volunteer-Friendly Church Culture* (Loveland, CO: Group, 2004), 47–53.

contributions to make. Or the problem may be more general, such as not knowing what sort of behavior to expect from other team members. A team covenant can correct this situation. George Cladis describes the covenant he developed with his church staff in Darien, Connecticut. It included these promises: (1) intentionally encourage and bless one another; (2) disagree openly, avoiding triangulation and speaking unkindly of others; and (3) like the potter and the clay, be willing to be molded and changed.[6]

Talking while we work not only sustains us but may actually change us in the process. Ann Morisy, who works with British churches seeking to expand their outreach, sees dialogue as central to community ministry. She writes, "The essence of dialogue is that each person who is party to the communication is open to the possibility of being changed by the testimony of the other."[7] Talk does more work than we give it credit for.

6. George Cladis, *Leading the Team-Based Church* (San Francisco: Jossey-Bass, 1999), 160–61.
7. Ann Morisey, *Beyond the Good Samaritan: Community Ministry and Mission* (London: Bloomsbury, 2003), 65.

18

Start a Conversation with a Stranger

We hold conversations all the time yet rarely think about it. Yet talking with others offers a gateway to understanding others who live in our community. In a real sense, conversation can help us fulfill Jesus's commandment to "love your neighbor as yourself" because of the opportunity it offers to appreciate what we share in common with people from different cultural, racial, or economic backgrounds.

Sherry Turkle, in her book *Reclaiming Conversation*, worries that we may be losing the art of conversation. A specialist in social-media use, Turkle expresses concerns about the "flight from conversation" occasioned by cell-phone use, especially texting and social media. We need to reclaim the art of conversation, she asserts, because "It's where we develop the capacity for empathy." In interviewing college students to determine patterns of texting, she came to an unexpected discovery: fewer conversations were taking place. The presence of a phone changes the pattern of communication. If we think we might be interrupted, we keep our conversations lighter.[1]

Key choices, sometimes unconscious, come into play when we talk with anyone, including strangers. K. Sellon and Daniel P. Smith, church consultants, train church leaders on how to become more purposeful in relationships with others. Undergirding their approach is Jesus's commandment to "love your neighbor," a love that goes beyond emotion to include our intention and stance toward others. As we meet and get to know someone, or when we go deeper to establish a relationship with someone, six choices confront us:

1. What do I want my relationship with this person to be like?
2. What attitudes and values do I want to honor when I'm with this person?
3. What must I let go of in order to turn toward this person?
4. What is the goodness in this person that I will see and trust?
5. How will I acknowledge to the person the holy goodness that I see in them?
6. What will I dare to ask of this person?[2]

1. Sherry Turkle, *Reclaiming Conversation: The Power of Talk in a Digital Age* (New York: Penguin, 2015), 3, 21.
2. Mary K. Sellon and Daniel P. Smith, *Practicing Right Relationship* (Lanham, MD: Rowman & Littlefield, 2005), 69.

In preparing to enter into a conversation with someone, acknowledging that we have choices may help us to bring about the results we want to achieve.

Yet to get down to brass tacks, what can you actually say when first meeting someone? Nicholas Boothman, a specialist in face-to-face communication, suggests opening your body and attitude. Avoid defensive gestures such as crossed arms or clenched fists, which communicate a reluctance to engage. Be the first person to make eye contact and also be the first person to smile. Boothman employs a great term for this: to "beam," as if embodying a shining light that reflects a positive attitude. Say "hello," "hi," or whatever seems appropriate, and shake the person's hand if it feels right. He also suggests leaning toward the person. "This action can be an almost imperceptible tilt to subtly indicate your interest and openness."[3]

What if you share space with someone you don't know? One method: make a statement about your location or about the occasion you share. Small talk about the weather certainly fits the bill, but it's often possible to be more specific. Follow this up with an open-ended question, something that does not readily admit of a yes or no answer. Such open-ended questions often begin with "who, what, when, where, why, or how?" and invite someone to share something about how they are feeling or experiencing the moment.[4] Then listen! And let the person know you are listening through your expression.

3. Nicholas Boothman, *How to Make People Like You in 90 Seconds or Less* (New York: Workman, 2008), 14–16.
4. Boothman, *How to Make People Like You*, 92.

What if the stranger appears to be homeless? Winston Ross, a journalist, interviewed the homeless and those who work with them about this question. He suggest five conversation starters.

"I don't have money, but is there another way I can help you?" This works especially well if you are uncomfortable giving cash or do not have any to offer. Often there is one specific thing that can help a person in need. A homeless advocate in San Francisco often hands out pairs of socks or granola bars along with her agency's business card.

"Did you catch the game?" Athletic events can often be seen on televisions at shelters. Talking about sports can be interesting, and it equalizes the conversation in the sense that anyone of whatever class can participate on the same footing.

"Good morning." Acknowledging someone by making eye contact and offering a greeting seems so basic, yet it can make a difference. As a homeless advocate in San Antonio, Texas, puts it, "The non-homeless person almost never looks the homeless in the eye. If you just look a person in the eye and sort of nod, it's the most respectful thing you can ever do."

"How are you doing? Would you like to talk?" The good thing about these questions is that they are open-ended, offering the person a choice of whether to go deeper. Joe, a homeless person in Portland, Oregon, says not to be surprised if someone is not interested in chatting. "You're getting into people's personal lives. Maybe they don't want to discuss that with a stranger." If the conversation continues, it can serve

a real need—reducing social isolation that can be especially acute for those who live on the streets.

"I will keep you in my thoughts." This phrase, or something like it, conveys respect and caring. If you are comfortable with this, offer to pray with someone. Sean Gasson, a thirty-two-year-old homeless man in Portland, says, "When someone prays with you, it just makes you feel a little better."

While talking with others may seem as natural as riding a bicycle, even this is learned behavior. It never hurts to review the basics of something so important and potentially life giving. If Sherry Turkle is right that conversations are "where we develop the capacity for empathy," then we simply cannot have too many of them, even if it's only to pass the time of day with a stranger.

19

Accompany Someone in Need

Accompanying someone who feels vulnerable or threatened can offer something intangible—the gift of reassurance. Though most associated with immigrants facing deportation, accompaniment also takes place whenever we make a commitment to walk with someone struggling with poverty or addiction. Such actions hold promise for building relationships across race and class.

Some churches have begun accompanying immigrants faced with the possibility of deportation by US Immigration and Customs Enforcement (ICE). The experience can be daunting, and it is complicated by the fact that many immigrants lack basic English proficiency. Walking with such a person may not provide all the answers for them, but it may render the process a bit more humane.

Interfaith groups in New York City, Chicago, Los Angeles, and other cities have responded to recent restrictions in immigration policy by calling for volunteers to accompany immigrants facing detention. These "friends" of the detained are typically not lawyers and do not offer legal advice. Instead, they provide something more simple and intangible—a ministry of presence and of bearing witness for individuals who might be forced to face government attorneys alone, given that the Sixth Amendment does not guarantee immigrants the right to a lawyer.

The New Sanctuary Movement of New York City, an interfaith network of congregations, organizations, and individuals helping those facing deportation, describes places where church leaders can be present with immigrants: (1) at check-ins required by ICE; (2) at court hearings for individuals who have not been detained; and (3) at court hearings for those who have already been detained. Sara Gozalo, an organizer with New Sanctuary, described this kind of advocacy as "advocacy without confrontation" at a volunteer training held for sixty persons. "Even if you feel like you're not doing anything, your presence there means a lot. I promise you. It's much harder to deport someone when people are watching."[1]

In addition to being present at hearings, the US Council of Catholic Bishops suggests other ways to support immigrants, such as accompanying families with children to school and assisting with enrollment, or sponsoring an open house for parents, teachers, and administrators to discuss ways to

1. Katrina Shakarian, "As Trump Pushes Deportations, Volunteers Intensify Immigrant-Accompaniment Program," *Gotham Gazette*, January 8, 2018, https://tinyurl.com/y6us4rtf.

help. Beyond this, build a relationship with the Department of Homeland Security office by attending Community Relations Meetings sponsored by the agency. Finally, help immigrants find lawyers by holding information sessions about reputable immigration service providers.[2]

Accompaniment methods can be used in support of ministry with prisoners. For instance, St. Anne's Catholic Community, thirty-two miles northwest of Chicago, became involved in a program for mothers in prison that allows these mothers the opportunity to visit with their children. Sponsored by the Lutheran Social Services of Illinois, the "Visits to Mom" program provides free transportation to children whose mothers are incarcerated. For volunteers from St. Anne's, this typically translates into an eleven- or twelve-hour day due to the drive required to and from the Decatur and Logan Correctional Centers. That's a three-hour round trip from Barrington to Chicago and a five-hour round trip to and from the two prisons. These visits often represented the only chance for many of these mothers, many of them serving time for drug offenses, to see their children.[3]

Accompaniment, or the ministry of presence and support, can be expressed through the ministry of mentoring or advising for persons struggling with poverty or addiction. The West Side Campaign against Hunger (WCAH), located in the basement of the St. Paul and St. Andrew United

2. United States Conference of Catholic Bishops,"10 Things You Can Do to Accompany Immigrants," May 2017, https://tinyurl.com/ycmyrguv.
3. Victor Claman and David Butler, *Acting on Your Faith: Congregations Making a Difference* (Boston: Insights, 1994), 21.

Methodist Church in upper Manhattan, offers a supermarket-style food pantry that allows customers to choose which foods they will receive. Every new customer can receive the service of a social-service counselor who explains how to shop, how to apply for a health plan, how to find a doctor, and how to determine eligibility for federal programs such as SNAP (Supplemental Nutrition Assistance Program); Women, Infants, and Children (WIC); and Free and Reduced Price School Meals, as well as the pantry's own programs. Mentoring may also lead customers to job training and classes in General Educational Development (GED) and English as a Second Language (ESL). WHAC's social-service counseling metaphorically "walks with" customers who might be confused by the complicated web of services available.

Accompaniment can have a profound impact for both the accompanist and the one accompanied. Grace Yukich, a sociologist, documents this in a study of the New Sanctuary Movement's earlier work with immigrants in New York City in 2008. One woman, a member of the Lutheran Church of the Good Shepherd in Brooklyn, testified to a group of immigrant-support activists about her newfound faith that resulted from an accompaniment experience. She had been accompanying a Chinese couple to check-ins for several months. Though she had little prior experience with immigrants, she found her faith commitment deepening as she attended church with the couple, met occasionally at a restaurant to check on the couple's situation, and also went with them to periodic check-in meetings with immigration officials. Though never particularly committed to immigrant rights before, she began to experience a newfound sense of faith. "This is the first time I have felt there was a purpose to being a Christian."[4]

When we accompany others in need, we make a commitment to be present and bear witness to their struggle. In doing so, we move debates over immigration policy and alleviating poverty from the realm of abstraction to the reality of the lives of real families that are affected.

4. Grace Yukich, *One Family under God: Immigration Politics and Progressive Religion in America* (New York: Oxford University Press, 2013), 74.

20

Encourage and Support Personal Development

Personal development strategies can be easily overlooked. Such development tools aim at improving the physical, financial, or emotional condition of individuals by using information, skills, and power. Examples include job counseling for returning military veterans, tutoring for school children in economically challenged communities, mentoring for gang members trying to leave their old lives behind, financial counseling related to debt reduction and home ownership, business education for entrepreneurs, English as a Second Language (ESL) courses for immigrants, and substance abuse rehabilitation, such as Alcoholics Anonymous and other Twelve-Step recovery programs. Such strategies tend to be indirect, seeking social change by addressing the underlying reasons for social and economic difficulties. As a Presbyterian pastor in Philadelphia put it, speaking of people struggling with unemployment: "Our main concern is there's no hope. There's no hope because they're unemployed. They're unemployed because they're uneducated."[1] While not the only path toward social change, personal development can lay the foundation for long-term change.

Such methods take time. This might account for the fact that such ministries appear to be less popular than ministries that provide for physical needs. A national study of congregational outreach by Hartford Seminary reports that the three most common ministries provided by congregations involve providing cash, food, or clothing assistance with roughly three-quarters of US churches involved in at least one of these ministries. By contrast, about one-third of congregations nationwide offer programs that develop individuals. One reason for the disparity might be that building relationships takes more time than offering food, clothing, and cash, programs that more easily accommodate the limited schedules of busy "plug-in volunteers."[2]

Nevertheless, personal-development ministries may have a more lasting impact than programs that simply address physical needs. Heidi Unruh and Ron Sider, in their study of faith-based outreach in Philadelphia, observe, "These ministries have an undercurrent of empowerment that transcends the immediate provision of tangible aid such as food and clothing."[3] Food programs aim at hunger, while empower-

1. Heidi Unruh and Ronald Sider, *Saving Souls, Serving Society: Understanding the Faith Factor in Church-Based Social Ministry* (New York: Oxford University Press, 2005), 31.
2. Unruh and Sider, *Saving Souls*, 32.

ment programs aim at something more intangible—strengthening the individual's heart, mind, and soul. This implies a role for faith and a spiritual element, something churches are better positioned to address than most social-service agencies. Pastor Donna Jones describes the importance of faith for participants in Transitional Journey, a program sponsored by Cookman United Methodist Church that provides life-skills training, GED instruction, computer classes, job placement, and follow-up services to about thirty women on public assistance. Pastor Donna Jones says, "When you're talking about people restoration, without the hope that comes from faith, I don't see that it's possible."[4]

Though the personal-development approach starts with the individual, it need not end there. For example, Circles USA (see "Prepare through Study," chap. 7) centers its training on personal financial education, leadership development training, one-on-one mentoring, and group support. However, once a month, Circles chapters hold a "Big Picture" meeting focused on public policy changes necessary to alleviate poverty. The personal and the political can go together. Bishop Grannum, pastor at New Covenant Baptist Church in Philadelphia, offered his view of the difference spiritual empowerment can make. Heidi Unruh describes a sermon he preached criticizing a Supreme Court decision dismantling affirmative action. "Yet even within an unjust system, he preached, Christians can experience an inner, spiritual

3. Unruh and Sider, *Saving Souls*, 31.
4. Unruh and Sider, *Saving Souls*, 202.

empowerment that eventually influences their external circumstances. People can't stop you in the street because your car looks too good or because they don't like the color of the person who's driving the new car. . . . But no one can take away what is in you. It's called empowerment." In Bishop Grannum's view, the church does not confront racial injustice directly but frees individuals to confront these systems themselves. "You will still have to live with the system on your back . . . ," but empowered by Jesus, "you will defy the system."[5]

The spiritual element of personal development makes it distinct from programs of food, clothing, and cash assistance. By their very nature, counseling, recovery programs, and other educational methods lend themselves to the hope of spiritual transformation for the student.

For example, Homeboy Industries helps gang members make a new life for themselves.

Founded in 1992 by Father Gregory Boyle, a Roman Catholic priest, the ministry seeks to integrate gang members into society. Started in an abandoned bakery across the street from the parish served by Father Boyle, Homeboy Industries employs 250 former gang members, one of the largest gang intervention programs in the country.

As gang members go through the program, they are expected to make changes both physically and spiritually, moving from "shaved to saved" and from gang tattoos, drug addiction, emaciated weight, oversized clothes, shaved heads,

5. Unruh and Sider, *Saving Souls*, 62.

and aggressive body language to tattoo removal, drug abstinence, abundant eating, dress clothes, longer hairstyle, and affectionate body language. In return, these former gang members receive job training. The program's motto is "Jobs, not Jail," and the former gang members work in the bakery, café, silk-screening shop, and landscaping business, all operated by Homeboy Industries.

Gang members undergo spiritual changes as well. Homeboy Industries combines a "therapeutic approach" to recovery with an emphasis on spirituality. Former gang members utilize legal services, tattoo removal, and self-help workshops, often using therapeutic language to describe their spiritual journey. Most classes are modeled on the method of twelve-step programs, with conversation playing a key role as participants share about their spiritual lives during "check-in" time at the beginning. Every workday opens with Father Boyle or a surrogate offering a story for spiritual reflection and inspiration. Homeboy's "spiritual ecumenism" emphasizes right living more than adherence to a specific set of doctrines, and yoga and meditation are the favorite spiritual practices.[6]

Personal development strategies merit a second look. While food, clothing, and cash assistance offer more immediate help, programs like counseling, ESL classes, and gang recovery offer something more long-range—the opportunity to learn, grow, and develop into someone who can fully take part in the life of a citizen.

6. Edward Orozco Flores, *God's Gangs: Barrio Ministry, Masculinity, and Gang Recovery* (New York: New York University Press, 2014), 88–108, 168–90.

21

Hold a One-on-One Interview

"Sanity hangs on the thin thread of conversation," wrote the poet W. H. Auden. In addition to its mental-health benefits, holding conversations with our neighbors can provide vital information about the community. A one-on-one interview takes the process a step further. By structuring the conversation around a set of questions prepared in advance, we can keep the focus on matters related to our community work.

Joy Skjegstad, who consults with churches in the area of community ministry, finds that many churches prefer to skip the listening step and simply launch into a new community project. "It is faster to plan programming without it, because listening takes time—more time than just plotting out what is already in your head."[1] Church leaders also tell her they find it intimidating to meet people they do not know, especially

1. Joy F. Skjegstad, *Seven Models for Community Ministry* (Valley Forge, PA: Judson, 2013), 12.

when people in the community come from different ethnic, cultural, socioeconomic, or religious backgrounds than church members. Finally, Skjegstad suspects that some church leaders do not want new information to contradict their long-held assumptions. "Particularly for congregations that have enjoyed success and that are admired by others as leaders in ministry, community listening can be a humbling process. People in the community may tell you things you don't want to hear."[2]

Faith-based community organizers consider one-on-one interviews to be an important tool in organizing for social change. Of course, many organizers share an activist bent that prioritizes bold actions to mobilize their congregations for the struggle. Yet the Reverend Dennis Jacobsen, an Evangelical Lutheran pastor and community organizer, observes that organizing efforts can falter without a strong dose of relationship building, and the one-on-one interview serves as a primary way to achieve this goal. "Organizing misses its calling," Jacobsen writes, "when it becomes a swirl of frenetic activity, addicted to issues and actions, running past and over human beings. One-on-ones slow things down, restore needed focus, and serve as a reminder of the human dimension of this work."[3]

Interviews come in three styles—structured, unstructured, and semi-structured. If you want to get to know the person or community, try an *unstructured interview*. Start with a broad

2. Skjegstad, *Seven Models for Community Ministry*, 13.
3. Dennis Jacobsen, *Doing Justice: Congregations and Community Organizing* (Minneapolis: Fortress Press, 2001), 60.

question about your interviewee's experience and then just let the conversation flow in whatever direction it will. However, if you want to assess a community's needs or analyze a particular problem, a *structured interview* may serve the purpose better. In this case, ask questions about specific issues, possibly even limiting the options to yes or no answers. At the extreme end of the structured format, this interview may resemble a verbal questionnaire more than a free-flowing conversation. The *semi-structured interview* strikes a compromise between the two styles, utilizing predetermined questions while allowing respondents to use whatever language they are most comfortable with or allowing them to wander from the topic as it suits them.[4]

A basic unstructured interview may be the easiest type of interview to accomplish. Andrea Fontana and James Frey, both social scientists, offer the following seven steps for preparing for and carrying out an interview.

1. *Access the setting*. How do you "get in to" wherever the interview will take place? This question must be asked because interviews typically do not take place on your own turf but in the field. How you access the setting depends on the group you are studying. When these social-scientist authors conducted research about nude beaches for a book they were writing, accessing the setting required disrobing and strolling casually on the beach. Yet another researcher-author had to buy a motorcycle and hang out where Hell's

4. Scott Thumma, "Methods for Studying Congregations," in *Studying Congregations: A New Handbook*, ed. Nancy Ammerman et al. (Nashville: Abingdon, 1998), 206.

Angels were known to gather in order to interview them for a book they were writing. While these may be extreme cases, they illustrate a point: in order to interview someone, you need to enter their setting, not invite them to yours.

2. *Understand the language and culture.* An interpreter may help you understand the person you interview, but that is no guarantee you will understand the culture. If you are non-Hispanic, it may feel puzzling and uncomfortable to answer a volley of questions about whether you are married, and if so, how long and with how many children. Yet the family holds a key place in Hispanic culture. Ignoring this reality may result in "mistranslation" even if you have a great interpreter.

3. *Decide how to present yourself.* Do you dress up or dress down? How you dress may be subject to misunderstanding. Dressing up may create suspicion among some undocumented immigrants, who might believe that you represent the federal government. Likewise, dressing up with factory workers might convey the sense that you work for management. On the other hand, dressing down can be equally misunderstood. If you are interviewing parishioners in a Sunday morning church setting at a black church, dressing down might be seen as disrespectful to God. So, it all depends. A best practice in many cases might be this: try to match your dress to that of the person being interviewed.

4. *Locate an informant.* You may need someone who can act as a guide to the local culture and its distinctive idiom. In one low-income neighborhood in a city I know, a woman known as "the mayor" of the neighborhood regularly welcomes her neighbors for evening gatherings on her front porch. She would qualify as a good informant.

5. *Gain trust.* Gaining trust may serve as an important prelude to getting someone to talk about themselves. Trust may not be such an issue for someone known to be outspoken on public issues, but it may be more essential if the interview concerns sensitive matters such as sexual behavior or personal finance.

6. *Establish rapport.* Developing a strong connection, a sense of ease between you and the person you interview, can open the door to a deeper dive into important information. Establishing rapport might not be crucial in some cases. For example, if your goal is to survey as many people as possible on a given issue, establishing a strong connection might take too long. Neighborhood surveys do not typically require deep rapport with everyone you poll.

7. *Collect the data.* How will you record what you find out? The most thorough techniques (video or audio), may seem the best, yet they might be the most intrusive. In some cases, note-taking may even have an off-putting effect. In this case, you might try taking mental notes and writing it up later in private soon afterward. Best practices for collecting data include (1) taking notes regularly and writing them down immediately; (2) writing everything down even if it seems

unimportant; (3) trying to be inconspicuous in talking notes; and (4) analyzing your notes often.[5]

Broadway United Methodist Church in Indianapolis offers one example of how to conduct interviews in the neighborhood. The church hired a "roving listener" to wander through the neighborhood and spend time with people he encountered. This person focused not on neighbors' needs but on their gifts, passions, and hopes for the community. The interviewer asked these questions:

- "What three things do you do well enough that you could teach others how to do them?"
- "What three things would you like to learn?"
- "Who, besides God and me, is going with you along the way?"[6]

Nothing beats a direct one-on-one interview for learning about the community and building relationships. Such interviews offer us a chance to get to know our neighbors in their own settings. Sometimes we may be surprised by their willingness to express their faith in personal, direct terms outside the worship setting. One researcher, who conducted one-on-one interviews for a faith-based community organization, tells about a neighbor who wanted to pray for her interviewer

5. Andrea Fontana and James Frey, "The Interview," in *Handbook of Qualitative Research*, ed. Norman Denzin and Yvonne Lincoln, 2nd ed. (Thousand Oaks, CA: Sage, 2000), 654–56.
6. Paul Nixon, *Fling Open the Doors: Giving the Church Away to the Community* (Nashville: Abingdon, 2002), 22–23.

as the conversation concluded. “Lord Jesus,” she said, “help us work together to change things here. Thank you for this new friend. Give us your Spirit and your power, and we will turn this city around for [his son] and for everybody.”[7]

7. Richard Wood, *Faith in Action: Religion, Race, and Democratic Organizing in America* (Chicago: University of Chicago Press, 2002), 165.

PART V

Collaborative Tools

22

Engage in Public Policy Deliberation

Talking politics may seem like a great way to spoil a conversation, yet issues of public concern are often the very places where your ministry engages the community. To address such concerns, church leaders can hold forums on public issues of the day, as long as these discussions are well structured and fair. The meeting must be designed so that everyone gets a chance to speak, others listen respectfully, and the best solutions emerge. In other words, it must be deliberative. The term *deliberation* may seem a little opaque, but it describes a specific style of conversation in which "citizens, public officials, public employees, and other stakeholders interact in small-group sessions where they share experiences, consider a range of policy options, and decide together what should be done."[1]

Deliberative work has become increasingly important given the sorry state of political discourse these days. Whether at the federal, state, or local level, policymaking has become an arena of deadlock and dysfunction. Ordinary citizens often feel marginalized when it comes to political decision-making as issues get framed in the media and by elected officials in a way that leads to divisiveness. Often, it seems, elected officials and even voters make poor decisions because they have not allowed the time to discuss the options together.[2] Deliberative forums are a tool that churches can use to help communities grapple with these issues in a more purposeful and enlightened way.

Deliberative forums go by a variety of different names and take a variety of forms. Some processes were named by the people or organizations that developed them, such as Public Issues Forums, Dialogue-to-Change Programs, and 21st Century Town Meetings. Or you may hear them under more generic rubrics like "community conversations," "study circle programs," or "roundtables." A few of the key organizations promoting deliberative forums are Everyday Democracy, the Kettering Foundation, Public Agenda, and the National Institute for Civil Discourse. What these forums have in common is a highly structured process that usually requires some advance preparation from the participants and aims at securing a diverse group of people.[3]

1. Tina Nabatchi and Matt Leighninger, *Public Participation for the 21st Century* (Hoboken, NJ: Jossey-Bass, 2015), 276.
2. *What Does the Kettering Foundation Do?* (Dayton, OH: Kettering Foundation, 2018).
3. Tina Nabatchi and Matt Leighninger, *Public Participation,* 276–77.

Deliberative work tends to be exploratory and open to revision. The meeting must be designed so that everyone gets a chance to speak, listen respectfully, and move toward understanding so that some common ground or possible solutions emerge. For this reason, the printed four-page guides for National Issues Forums always present three different and sharply defined policy options and then ask participants to examine with the options together, keeping in mind the trade-offs or disadvantages implicit in each one. Hard tactics have no place in deliberative work.

Deliberative forums can be employed when rhetoric has spiraled out of control. For example, two pastors in Oak Ridge, Tennessee, joined forces in 2015 in response to the heated public debate over police violence and community safety. Oak Ridge has been dubbed "The Secret City" in reference to its origins in the 1940s as a community for workers in the federally sponsored Manhattan Project, which built the first atomic bomb. Over time this city of twenty-nine thousand has become increasingly diverse (white, 83 percent; African American, 8 percent; Hispanic, 4 percent; and Asian American, 2 percent). In the summer of 2015, the largely white Oak Ridge Unitarian Universalist Church responded to widespread outrage over police violence nationwide by posting a message on its electronic sign: Black Lives Matter. When the pastor, the Reverend Jake Morrill, began receiving death threats, he called a meeting with his colleague, the Reverend Derrick Hammond, pastor of Oak Valley Baptist Church, a largely African American congregation in the city.

At that meeting, which was also attended by a Roman Catholic priest and the city's chief of police, the group decided to take the sign down and to host a series of three public forums called "Community Matters."

Though not acquainted with the term *deliberation* at the time, the group managed to design its own process for discussing the community's issues fairly and in depth. The process aimed to (1) identify the issues of most concern to the community, (2) do research using quantitative data that would offer an objective basis for understanding the concern, (3) identify resources that might improve the situation, and (4) resolve the issue by taking collective action. The ground rules were simple. Participants were to (1) speak as an individual, not as a representative of a group, (2) speak to concerns without laying blame or personal attacks, and (3) "remember there is no room for disrespect."[4]

The Reverend R. Gregg Kaufman, an Evangelical Lutheran pastor in Jacksonville, Florida, has begun using one type of process—the deliberative dialogue—to introduce civil discourse to church groups. A few months before the presidential election in 2016, Kaufman held a forum at St. John's Episcopal Cathedral on the topic of political dysfunction. Using a guide designed by the National Issues Forum Institute, *Political Fix: How Can We Get American Politics Back on Track?*, Kaufman laid out the process for the group.

4. Derrick Hammond, "Employing Democratic Practices to Address Community Forum Concerns," presented to the Kettering Foundation, October 20–21, 2016.

First, everyone present was invited to speak of a personal stake they had in the issue. Next Kaufman presented ground rules that emphasized listening and respect. Then he added a twist: no talk about the Trump/Pence or Clinton/Kaine presidential tickets. The goal was to find ways to talk about the political dysfunction and solutions to the problem in a way that encouraged respectful speaking and listening. Discussing politics with strangers can be intimidating, even with topics that may appear easy to reach consensus about, such as the need for reducing political dysfunction. Some participants had arrived at the meeting tense, expecting heated arguments. Before the discussion got very far along, however, the tenor of the group began to shift. "Speech that was like shaky steps on thin ice began to take on the feel of a driveway basketball game," according to an observer who later wrote about the evening. Kaufman has held over a dozen such forums in the Jacksonville area, with most of them using churches as sponsors or venues.[5]

"One who spares words is knowledgeable; one who is cool in spirit has understanding" (Prov 17:27). Cool speech can be learned. Group discussion does not have to be twisted by anger or marred by disrespect. Deliberation is possible, even concerning controversial matters such as immigration, community policing, or gun violence. By hosting forums, church leaders can offer a space where difficult issues get raised and, though perhaps not resolved, at least considered respectfully

5. Linell Ajello, "Out of the Shadows of Polarization," *Kettering Review* 34, no. 1 (Fall 2017): 23–29.

and fairly. Along the way, churches might help their members, as well as their neighbors, learn how to be better citizens.

23

Invite Someone to Share the Life of Faith

Imagine inviting someone to church. What a novel idea! Now imagine inviting someone who struggles to make ends meet and keep a roof overhead. Church leaders could "go the second mile" with people they serve by bringing them along with them to church. Why doesn't this happen more often?

Church growth can be built on a missional worship model more effectively than an attractional model, which seeks to draw people based primarily on the brilliance of their worship offerings. In the missional model, churches grow through the expansion of the church leader's "personal mission field," which, if you work on a regular basis with the economically marginalized, includes them as well. In this model, you are not inviting them into worship but to share the life of faith.[1]

1. Cathy Townley, *Missional Worship: Increasing Attendance and Expanding the Boundaries of Your Church* (St. Louis: Chalice, 2011), 23–25.

Be aware that a simple verbal invitation may not be enough. This proved to be the case for a United Methodist church in the downtown section of Troy, New York. The church, known for its commitment to social justice, holds a block party every year for the neighbors. This city of fifty thousand, located near the state capital of Albany, experiences the economic problems of many cities in the northeast, including a low tax base, limited job opportunities, building vacancies, homelessness, drug use, and crime. Given its location within blocks of low-income and subsidized residential housing, the church would appear to be well-positioned to serve those in economic need. The church's annual block party, held in September, offers free lunch, a concert, and children's activities for the neighbors. While noting the large attendance at one of its block parties, a church leader lamented that none of those who attended bothered to follow up on his invitation to attend church on Sunday. "I have invited many of them, yet no one ever shows up."

What could have gone wrong? Perhaps this leader had not taken enough time to make a genuine connection with those he invited, showing an interest in their lives, before asking them to be part of a new community. Or perhaps he failed to take into account the shame often felt by those who receive free food, or the perception held by others that church represents a solidly middle-class place and is therefore not for them.

Low-income residents face particular challenges not faced by well-resourced, middle-class parishioners. Susan Crawford

Sullivan, a sociologist, interviewed forty-five mothers on public assistance about their faith life. Though faith and spiritual practices mattered deeply to these mothers, many of them had given up on church. Many expressed frustrations about their inability to secure transportation. One mother, Elisa, used to receive rides from a family in her Pentecostal church, but then the rides stopped, and it was too far to walk. Others, such as Aletta, experienced housing instability. As a twenty-two-year-old black/Latina mother of three young children, Aletta had to quit attending her Seventh Day Adventist Church twice a week when she and her husband moved out of the neighborhood and into a long-term transitional housing shelter. She cited rules such as curfews at her housing shelter as an obstacle. "Once I get my apartment, we will attend church. But in the shelters, it's kind of hard. You've got to do a lot of things, follow the rules. So, I don't really attend church right now." Others experienced stigma. Fully one-third of the forty-five mothers Sullivan interviewed told her they felt stigmatized for being poor and being on welfare. Whether the judgmental attitudes of others were real or perceived, these mothers felt ashamed to be on welfare. Shantelle said, "Growing up in church, most of the people there were working people. They wasn't on welfare." For others, it came down to feeling poorly dressed. Some women felt that church is more appropriate for middle-class persons, not the poor. Still others had been publicly criticized. Most women in her study had experienced criticism or discrimination in other places, such as welfare offices or stores, or when applying for a job or attending health clinics. Those who had worked previously, prior to going on welfare, felt the sting even more intensely.[2]

How can we take into account the real-life experience of the marginalized even as we invite them to church? A San Antonio, Texas, church offers a model. The leaders of Travis Park United Methodist Church struggled for years to revive their dying, downtown church located in a neighborhood with economic need. The leaders felt exhausted by their efforts to revive the congregation. According to the pastor, John Flowers, the turnaround began when the youth group initiated "Cafe Corazon" (Spanish for "heart"), a breakfast program for anyone who was hungry, regardless of the ability to pay. After five years, the Sunday morning program averaged 120 volunteers and fed 200 people. At the same time, church leaders spent two years studying books on how to revitalize the congregation, a crucial step in achieving change.[3] At one point, the church began making changes to its worship offerings, with organ and choral music at the early service and contemporary music at 11:00 a.m. At this point, a number of members left the church, citing their discomfort with either the worship changes or its ministry to the poor. To emphasize the church's new commitments, worship lead-

2. Susan Crawford Sullivan, *Living Faith: Everyday Religion and Mothers in Poverty* (Chicago: University of Chicago Press, 2011), 157, 160–61.
3. Such books include Alice Mann, *Can Our Church Live?: Redeveloping Congregations in Decline* (Lanham, MD: Rowman & Littlefield, 2000); William T. McConnell, *Renew Your Congregation: Healing the Sick, Raising the Dead* (St. Louis: Chalice, 2007); and Jorge Acevedo, *Vital: Churches Changing Communities and the World* (Nashville: Abingdon, 2012).

ers framed the worship services using biblical stories about the marginalized. Finally, they decided to begin the process of systematically inviting the poor. "We first invited the homeless to come to worship. Then we began to tell them, one on one, that we needed them to be in church with us. We were too white, too privileged, and too churched to be real." After that, the numerical decline of the congregation was reversed, and the "spiritual apathy" disappeared.[4]

Inviting those we serve to worship with us would seem to be a natural outgrowth of Jesus's commandment, "You shall love your neighbor as yourself" (Matthew 23:39). Jesus assumes that self-interest motivates much of what we do, and he does not condemn it outright but asks that we consider our neighbor's interest as well as our own. With regard to worship, this means wanting others to get the same spiritual benefit we receive from worship. We can love others by inviting them to participate in our faith life.

4. John Flowers and Karen Vannoy, "Growing Mission with God's People on the Margins," *Net Results* (January/February 2004).

24

Organize a Block Party

If you want to get to know your community, try organizing a block party. It can be a great way to meet neighbors and develop friendships. Some neighborhoods feel more secure once the neighbors have become acquainted. A key goal of a block party, besides having fun, should be to build relationships among the strangers in our midst. Beyond this, consider developing a simple theme (such as a color or a holiday) or highlighting a social issue the community needs to mobilize around (such as saving the community garden). Here are seven steps for organizing a block party.[1]

Step 1: Have a Clear Goal

Most block parties have a general purpose: to enjoy music, food, conversation, games, or dance so that we can get to know our neighbors. Especially if it's the first party you are

1. Adapted from Benjamin Shepard, *Community Projects as Social Activism* (Thousand Oaks, CA: Sage, 2015), 20–23.

planning, this general purpose might be enough. You can have a theme as well, such as a focus on children, ethnic food, or a holiday. With a little imagination, the focus could become more specific. Is there a particular issue in the community that you want to highlight, such as schools, policing, parking, or community pride?

Step 2: Do a Little Research

Get in touch with your neighbors. Even before you set a time and date, talk one-on-one with people you know about a theme, or find someone who seems to know everyone in the neighborhood and ask for help with networking. Even if the party idea started with you, gather a group to help with organizing the event itself by addressing basic questions about planning, such as where, when, and for how long it will last. Ideally, you would ask for input from neighbors before selecting a theme or addressing a community issue.

Step 3: Invite Your Neighbors

In some neighborhoods, it may be possible to go door to door passing out flyers with the time, date, and location of the event. If not, consider using email, social media, neighborhood newsletters, or posters to get the word out. Have a media team ready to take photos or videos to communicate that this is not just a block party but a means of community change, such as saving the community garden.

Step 4: Mobilize People around Food

Food is central to a block party's success. If you want to increase participation and reduce the cost, a potluck meal may be the best way to go. As an alternative, organizers could hold a barbecue, buying supplies and asking people to reimburse them for it, or have everyone bring their own meat or veggies to grill. If it's a picnic, everyone would bring their own meal. Though it's a lot of work, you could ask people to indicate on a sign-up sheet what type of dish they are bringing. Then a week or so before the block party, have the worker in charge of food contact everyone to remind them to bring the dishes they signed up for. Some churches prefer to offer a free meal as a way of giving back to the community. In this case, it is important that no strings be attached. There must be only one message: "We care about our neighbors, and here is how we want to show it."

If you choose a community issue as your focus, consider using the visual arts—a banner, or perhaps musicians, dancers, or street performers—to communicate your ideas. Benjamin Shepard, a social worker and professor of human services at City University of New York, writes, "A well-selected banner or perhaps grass or chairs can transform a street corner into a living room or even a community garden. . . . Connect the visuals with the message of the party. Art is part of getting the ideas out there."[2] Consider drafting a press release that would go to blogs, social media, and other media outlets

2. Benjamin Shepard, *Community Projects*, 21–22.

to explain how the party connects to the campaign you are organizing.

Step 5: Add Music and Games to the Mix

Besides food and music, games are key ingredients to a successful party. If you are located in a park and children are a focus, consider summer picnic games like bean-bag tosses, relay races, sack games, and wheelbarrow games. If the street is your locale, then bicycle-decorating contests and scavenger hunts might be more appropriate. Add music, both live and recorded, to the mix, and be sure to provide a sturdy sound system. If young children are living near the party area, then plan to finish by 9:00 p.m.

Step 6: Stay Legal

Many municipalities require a permit if your block party will close down a street or redirect traffic, or if it will be located in a public park. If a public site is used, it will need to be cleaned up afterward. The best bet would be to check the city's website for information on requirements. If you plan to have music, pay attention to noise ordinances.

Step 7: Don't Be Afraid to Improvise

Even for relatively small-scale events, block parties require a lot of planning. It's important to prepare for the worst case. For example, do you know what to do in case of a medical emergency? Finally, the day arrives, and the party begins.

People arrive or not. There is enough food or not. It rains or not. In the end, block parties are a form of group play. Don't be afraid to improvise, and remember to have fun!

Whether the purpose is to get to know our neighbors or mobilize around a social issue, a block party can be an effective way to draw people out from behind locked doors, walls, and hedges. What better excuse than an outdoor event to roam from driveway to yard to sidewalk to street, rubbing shoulders with people we recognize but have never met? In order to know the community, we need to go out. A block party can break down the isolation a bit, offering a little fun along the way.

25

Play Serious Games

Church leaders who work hard to feed the hungry and clothe the naked may not feel they have time for games. Anyway, what good would it do? After all, poverty and inequality are not matters to be treated lightly, or so the thinking goes. Despite such stern attitudes, community engagement does not have to be drudgery.

What good do games do? First of all, they can make civic engagement more fun. Unfortunately, many people have come to expect civic involvement to be unsatisfying, and often with good reason. Josh Lerner, in *Making Democracy Fun*, believes most citizens see involvement in local government forums such as public hearings as comparable to eating spinach, which everyone claims is good for you, but nobody actually wants to eat. "For most people, democratic participation is relatively unappealing. It is boring, painful, and pointless." The opposite of this would be an engagement process that is fun.[1]

It's time for games to be taken seriously as a tool for community engagement. Games offer churches an enjoyable, satisfying way to deepen understanding of public issues. Serious games offer three benefits: they can (1) educate citizens about important community issues, (2) strengthen relationships between neighbors, and (3) help people work together to develop new solutions to longstanding problems. Serious games can be informative and fun at the same time.[2]

Games can strengthen relationships between neighbors. The Brady Faith Center in Syracuse, New York, provides an example of building relationships with low-income neighbors. The Brady Center offers a bicycle program for homeless persons. Residents of the city's shelters have the opportunity to explore the city on bike, often riding alongside middle managers working in the city's corporate towers. Andrew Lunetta, employed by a local shelter, started the program after he noticed that residents had to leave the shelter at 7:00 a.m. each morning and often had no place to go. He asked the Brady Center for space to gather them for coffee and board games. When spring arrived, it seemed better to go outside. For that reason, Lunetta, a bike enthusiast, started leading bike rides, which now happen three times a week. After ten rides, a person is allowed to keep the bike, helmet, and lock. Kevin Frank, executive director, said, "When we're on a bike together, we're all neighbors on the bike. We're all

1. Tina Nabatchi and Matt Leighninger, *Public Participation for 21st Century Democracy* (Hoboken, NJ: Jossey-Bass, 2015), 271.
2. Nabatchi and Leighinger, *Public Participation*, 271.

equal. We're all just friends. It's a chance to live community together."

While fun, the Brady Center's bike rides would probably not qualify as a game. Games typically are more structured than play. Game designers create a system that allows the players to engage in "artificial conflict" (that is, separate from real life). Second, game designers create rules that everyone must follow. Finally, the game must produce a measurable outcome, such as a score or reward. By contrast, play, such as bike riding, shooting hoops at a basketball court, or skateboarding in a public place, tends to be looser and more free form.[3] Both games and play can be immensely satisfying.

Games can educate citizens about important community issues. Poverty simulations provide an example of the civic-oriented game. Increasingly popular with churches concerned about economic inequality, The Community Action Poverty Simulation was developed by the Missouri Community Action Network as a way to raise awareness about the struggles poor people face and inspire solutions. This game seeks to help players understand what it would be like to live in poverty for a month.

At the start, players select an identity. The poverty simulation kit includes twenty-six brief profiles of families experiencing poverty. For example, you might be asked to play a nineteen-year-old mother who is a high-school dropout and unemployed. The young mother would like to go back to

3. Josh Lerner, *Making Democracy Fun: How Game Design Can Empower Citizens and Transform Politics* (Cambridge, MA: MIT Press, 2014), 13–15.

school and graduate, but she must care for a one-year-old son, the child of her former boyfriend. She rents a mobile home with a boyfriend who contributes toward half the cost, and she receives public assistance, including food stamps. But she gets no support from the child's father. While the boyfriend owns a car, the young mother does not own a phone.[4]

After everyone has selected a role, the clock begins. The poverty simulation takes place over four weeks, each session fifteen minutes long, in a room arranged to simulate a city or town complete with banks, stores, child-care providers, payday lenders, and local government agencies. Using props such as money, food stamps, and transportation cards, players must navigate their lives with limited resources, severe time constraints, and inadequate transportation. When time's up, a facilitator leads a discussion about the experience. In one simulation that took place in a church fellowship hall with about forty participants, the players shared afterward that although the game was brief, it was stressful and evoked surprisingly intense emotions, such as anger, frustration, panic, and even sadness.

Games can help people identify longstanding problems and work together to develop new solutions. Participatory budgeting offers a new method to get people involved in solving problems. It began in Porto Alegre, Brazil, in 1990 when the city invited communities to have a say in how community

4. Steve Inskeep, "A City Steps Up: Savannah Confronts Poverty," *Morning Edition*, National Public Radio, March 20, 2006, https://tinyurl.com/ybjb2ern.

dollars would be spent. The model has been used by fifteen hundred cities around the world, as well as schools, universities, housing authorities, businesses, and nonprofit organizations.[5] Budgeting can be a challenging process. Often experts or those who hold the purse strings control the process. In participatory budgeting, ordinary people get a say in the decision-making as they deliberate how to allocate funds.

Though methods vary widely, every participatory budgeting process shares these features: (1) a focus on a geographically defined area such as a neighborhood or district, (2) regularly scheduled meetings in each area to deliberate and make decisions, (3) activities scheduled to follow the budget cycle, and (4) a network of organizations or individuals who educate and mobilize others to take part.[6]

Above all, the process should be fun, and participants may be encouraged to get creative. In 2008, the Toronto Community Housing hosted "1.8 Day" to decide how to spend $1.8 million to upgrade its buildings and grounds. That Saturday, residents were asked to create displays promoting their idea for projects using the housing authority's funding. One proposal for a handicapped-accessible playground, called "Let All Children Play," used photos of children playing, text boxes to explain the project, and a three-dimensional playground model made of children's toys. Later that morning tenants were given five minutes to present on behalf of their project, and just for fun, a gong was struck to signal when

5. Nabatchi and Leighinger, *Public Participation for 21st Century Democracy*, 275.
6. Trevor Boutall, "Participatory Budgeting," Participedia, https://tinyurl.com/yakbbnfh.

time was up. At lunch everyone discussed the merits of the projects, and after lunch voting began via computer in a private room. Each delegate was allowed to cast ten votes, though delegates were not allowed to vote for their own project. "Most people left 1.8 Day smiling, whether or not their project won."[7]

How is participatory budgeting like a game? Recall the three elements of a game: conflict, rules, and measurable outcomes. In Toronto, *a set of rules* structured how issues were to be presented (using displays or verbal presentations) and how decisions were to be made (by talking together over lunch). *Conflict* occurred as players competed to design the most convincing display or presentation. Voting in the afternoon produced *measurable outcomes* as "winners" saw their favorite projects voted upon and either funded or not. Finally, like many games, the process left people smiling.

Participatory budgeting could be used internally by churches wanting to open up its own budget process to a broader group of members than simply the finance team. A similar process could be used by churches as a tool for community engagement. Imagine what would happen if, rather than offering donations of food, clothing, or cash, the church allocated an amount of money for the community, then invited residents into a process to determine how to spend it. That's participatory budgeting in a nutshell.

7. Lerner, *Making Democracy Fun*, 155–61.

26

Engaging in Long-Term Community Development

Engaging in long-term community development can feel quite different from offering help in a short-term crisis. Of course, emergencies happen, as any pastor will tell you who has received calls for cash assistance, food, or shelter. Poverty often presents itself as a crisis demanding immediate relief, writes Steve Corbett, a community development specialist. "*Relief* can be defined as the urgent and temporary provision of emergency aid to reduce immediate suffering from a natural or man-made crisis." The key to effectiveness lies in the term *temporary*. Unfortunately, extending relief over the long term can create dependence. As soon as the crisis ends, rehabilitation must begin, which "seeks to restore people and their communities to the positive elements of their pre-crisis conditions."[1]

Further down the road, development must begin, defined

by Corbett as "a process of ongoing change that moves all the people involved—both 'helpers' and 'helped'—closer to being in right relationship with God, self, others, and the rest of creation." Many American churches make the mistake of applying relief where rehabilitation or development would be more appropriate. To illustrate, he tells of his church's work at a homeless shelter. Church members would bring food and prepare a meal for shelter residents once a month, then return home satisfied at the help they had provided. Yet relief seemed the only thing they knew how to do, and they slathered it on. "We did everything short of spoon-feeding the men, never asking them to lift a finger in the entire process. A more developmental approach would have sought greater participation of these men in their own rehabilitation."[2]

Community development represents a more long-term approach to community engagement. One approach, asset-based community development, focuses on the resources required to rebuild a troubled community. This approach prioritizes asset-building over problem-solving (see "Determine the Problem to Be Solved," chap. 1), thereby energizing community actors to discover creative solutions for themselves.

The asset-based approach to community development involves five steps.[3]

1. Steve Corbett and Brian Fikkert, *When Helping Hurts: How to Alleviate Poverty without Hurting the Poor and Yourself* (Chicago: Moody, 2009), 104.
2. Corbett and Fikkert, *When Helping Hurts,* 111.
3. John Kretzmann and John McKnight, *Building Communities from the Inside Out* (Skokie, IL: ACTA, 1993), 9.

Step 1: Map the Entire Community's Assets

"Mapping" is a visual metaphor for taking an inventory of the different capacities that reside in the community. As you look across the landscape, start with individuals, and look for the "gifts of strangers" in your midst—persons who have capacities that rarely come into view. Move next to associations such as congregations or community organizations, and finally to institutions such as hospitals, parks, libraries, banks, businesses, or corporations. Develop the entire picture, or least aspire to it.

Step 2: Build Relationships

Relationship-building can start during the mapping process. Ask for help. Invite community members to engage in joint fact finding, perhaps through one-on-one conversations or community meetings. There is no single blueprint for building relationships, but people generally know the difference between being analyzed by an outsider and being engaged as an equal.

Step 3: Mobilize Assets for Economic Development and Information Sharing

Economically hard-hit communities can resemble Swiss cheese: the holes are apparent to those willing to look. If the problem is the lack of banks in the neighborhood or a crying need for grocery stores that provide inexpensive, fresh produce, then mobilizing assets might involve linking the existing institutions together, such as banks and grocery stores, to begin the process of economic renewal. Mobilizing gets you moving from talk to collective action.

Step 4: Convene the Community to Develop a Vision and a Plan

There are many models for community-wide strategic planning. No matter which strategic planning process you use, participants need to make three simple commitments: (1) begin with assets, (2) expand the table by inviting a wide variety of stakeholders, and (3) ground your planning, which can sometimes become starry-eyed in its optimism, in the reality of day-to-day problem-solving. Plant your feet firmly on the ground.

Step 5: Leverage Outside Resources

It should be obvious by now that an asset-based planning process must be driven from within the community by local residents. Nevertheless, leveraging outside resources (from government or business, for instance) can play a significant role, as long as it represents the final step and not the first one.[4] Try to avoid a situation where outside resources, such

4. For example, a Roman Catholic parish in Chicago partnered with a local hospital, hiring three staff persons with hospital funding, to develop health-related programs (Kretzmann and McKnight, *Building Communities*, 151). A Congregational church in Fairfield, Connecticut, partnered with a Jewish synagogue to purchase, for one dollar, the building that had formerly housed the city's police station, using it to house a homeless shelter (Victor N. Claman and David E. Butler, *Acting on Your Faith: Congregations Making a Difference*, with Jessica A. Boyatt [Boston: Insights, 1994], 29).

as a government funding or a foundation grant, serve as the cart that drives the horse.

In a sense, developing long-term partnerships represents the frontier of community engagement. Whether through community development or some other method, leaders need to practice good listening skills, focus on community resources, and think about how the project will enhance community sustainability five, ten, or fifteen years down the road. Doing so will ensure that the community receives lasting benefit.